Praise for *Motherh*

Maggie Combs has thrown a lifeline t[...] ability, she tackles some of the most p[...] today—and shows, instead, how to trad[...] and freedom of the gospel. *Motherhood W*[...] will encourage you, challenge you, help you, remind you, instruct you, and, most of all, point you to Jesus.

COURTNEY DOCTOR | Coordinator of Women's Initiatives, The Gospel Coalition; author of *From Garden to Glory: A Bible Study on the Bible's Story* and *Steadfast: A Devotional Bible Study on the Book of James*

Maggie has a gift for relieving unnecessary burdens in motherhood by applying the truth of the gospel. We're grateful for the way she consistently points moms to Christ.

EMILY JENSEN AND LAURA WIFLER | Cofounders of the Risen Motherhood ministry and coauthors of *Risen Motherhood: Gospel Hope for Everyday Moments*

If you are ready to find freedom from unhelpful expectations and replace them with hope-filled truth, then *Motherhood Without All the Rules* is the book you have been looking for. Filled with practical takeaways and transformational ideas, it is sure to gain a place at the top of your favorite books list.

MANDY ARIOTO | President and CEO, MOPS International

I wish I'd had *Motherhood Without All the Rules* when I first began my mothering journey. In it, Maggie Combs shows mothers how to walk in the grace of the gospel while prayerfully relying on the Holy Spirit. This book is a gift to mamas in any stage.

HUNTER BELESS | Host of the *Journeywomen* podcast

If there's one thing that can make a person's mind start to sizzle like an overheated engine, it's the heaping pile of unspoken rules the world offers on motherhood. What a relief this book was to my sizzling, overheated mind! Maggie's clear, engaging, and precise writing has a way of cutting through the most frenetic noise. I read this book during one of my most stressful seasons of motherhood, and though the words of most other books seemed to wiggle off the page, Maggie's words sang through clear as a bell. Even the most frazzled readers will come away feeling as if they've engaged in meaningful, freeing conversation with a friend while also suspecting they've been treated with sharp gospel truths by a doctor with an impeccable bedside manner. Maggie, thank you.

CAROLINE SAUNDERS | LifeWay author

As mothers, we so easily lose track of the simple gospel meant to fuel and sustain us. That's why I'm grateful for this resource! Maggie addresses the cultural messages in which we swim these days, pulling down false narratives and erecting beautiful God-oriented truths in their place. Read and let your heart be settled.

CHRISTINE HOOVER | Author of *With All Your Heart* and *Messy Beautiful Friendship*

Tired of spinning your wheels? In *Motherhood Without all the Rules*, Maggie Combs helps moms unhitch from burdensome motherhood maxims and mantras and paves the way forward with grace-fueled obedience. With the help of Maggie's disarming personal anecdotes, poignant observations, powerful biblical teaching, and practical action steps, you'll learn how to recognize and let go of (sometimes sneaky or subconscious) stressful standards and embrace the freedom and joy Christ offers to you in motherhood.

ABBEY WEDGEWORTH | Author of *Held: 31 Biblical Reflections on God's Comfort and Care in the Sorrow of Miscarriage*

Maggie invites moms to find freedom in the gospel from the overwhelming standards that the world sets up for motherhood. She offers words filled with gospel hope as well as practical tips for growing in godliness. Like a close friend, Maggie reminds moms that God is at work in them through this season of motherhood and exhorts them to grow in intimacy with God every step of their motherhood journey.

KRISTIN SCHMUCKER | Founder and CEO of The Daily Grace Co.

With the skill and humility that come only by experience, Maggie walks her readers through the experiences of life, exposing the lies we believe and replacing them with the good news of Jesus Christ. Those weighed down by the stress of worldly standards will find true and refreshing hope in these pages.

ERIC SCHUMACHER | Pastor, songwriter with Hymnicity, and coauthor of *Worthy: Celebrating the Value of Women*

Many of us moms don't realize how we're walking around, holding our breaths, tense under the weight of society's unwritten rules of motherhood. With gospel clarity, Maggie removes the burden brick by brick in *Motherhood Without All the Rules*. She slices through the appearance of wisdom the world offers moms with honesty, grace, and courage, bringing sighs of relief as she replaces the blinding burden with a paved path for our feet and equipping for the journey.

LAUREN WEIR | Biblical counselor and co-owner of Words Worth Noting

Reading this book has been like a warm conversation with a graceful friend who is speaking gospel truth directly to my wandering and forgetful heart. Mothering by the world's rules will stress and exhaust you, but embracing the truth of the gospel will lift your burden and make you whole in Christ. Open this book and take Maggie's hands as she invites you to make that trade.

BETSEY GOMEZ | Creative Director for the Spanish Outreach (ANC); leader of initiatives for young women in Spanish, *Joven Verdadera* podcast and blog

In *Motherhood Without All the Rules*, Maggie offers moms tangible gospel hope through sharing her experiences and struggles in motherhood and pointing moms to Jesus. She reminds us that the pressure is off to be the perfect mama because we have the perfect heavenly Father guiding us and providing for us. Instead of living for the kingdom of ourselves, where we are the "queens," Maggie offers us another kingdom to live for—the kingdom of God, ruled by our good and gracious King. This book is for all moms, and I guarantee, after reading these pages, you'll be refreshed and reminded of God's great grace and the freedom He freely gives.

GRETCHEN SAFFLES | Founder of Well-Watered Women

MOTHERHOOD WITHOUT ALL THE RULES

TRADING STRESSFUL STANDARDS FOR GOSPEL TRUTHS

MAGGIE COMBS

MOODY PUBLISHERS

CHICAGO

Unless otherwise indicated, Scripture quotations are from The ESV® Bible (The Holy Bible, English Standard Version®), copyright © 2001 by Crossway, a publishing ministry of Good News Publishers. Used by permission. All rights reserved.

Scripture quotations marked HCSB are taken from the Holman Christian Standard Bible®, copyright © 1999, 2000, 2002, 2003, 2009 by Holman Bible Publishers. Used by permission. Holman Christian Standard Bible®, Holman CSB®, and HCSB® are federally registered trademarks of Holman Bible Publishers.

Scripture quotations marked (NIV) are taken from the Holy Bible, New International Version®, NIV®. Copyright © 1973, 1978, 1984, 2011 by Biblica, Inc.™ Used by permission of Zondervan. All rights reserved worldwide. www.zondervan.com. The "NIV" and "New International Version" are trademarks registered in the United States Patent and Trademark Office by Biblica, Inc.™

Scripture quotations marked (NLT) are taken from the Holy Bible, New Living Translation, copyright ©1996, 2004, 2015 by Tyndale House Foundation. Used by permission of Tyndale House Publishers, a Division of Tyndale House Ministries, Carol Stream, Illinois 60188. All rights reserved.

All emphasis in Scripture has been added.

Names and details of some stories have been changed to protect the privacy of individuals.

Edited by Amanda Cleary Eastep
Interior Design: Erik M. Peterson
Cover Design: Faceout Studio
Cover illustration of brush strokes copyright © 2019 by it cool / Shutterstock (1437995162).
Cover illustration of gold foil copyright © 2019 by janniwet / Shutterstock (563600983).
All rights reserved for the above photos.
Author photo: Gina Zeidler

Library of Congress Cataloging-in-Publication Data

Names: Combs, Maggie, 1985- author.
Title: Motherhood without all the rules : trading stressful standards for
   gospel truths / Maggie Combs.
Description: Chicago : Moody Publishers, 2020. | Includes bibliographical
   references. | Summary: "Any mom who has tried to create a godly home for
   her family knows it doesn't happen automatically. Through books, blogs,
   and Instagram accounts, culture asserts that a good mom must follow
   certain standards and abide by certain rules if she wants what's best for
   her children. She must do everything she can-and she must do it all just
   right. Following the suggested steps and recommended rules may seem
   best, but what if we're missing the point? This is something Maggie
   Combs came to realize while seeking to be a good mom to her three sons.
   Though the world around us may have critical expectations and rules for
   mothering, Christ instead calls moms to an intimate, abiding
   relationship with a triune God. In Motherhood Without All the Rules,
   Maggie identifies the main "rules" moms today often feel pressured to
   follow and counters them with Gospel truth. You'll discover how the
   character of each member of the trinity practically impacts your role as
   a mom. Join Maggie in forgetting the rules, so that instead of being a
   good mom, you grow to become a holy mom"-- Provided by publisher.
Identifiers: LCCN 2020015685 (print) | LCCN 2020015686 (ebook) | ISBN
   9780802419453 (paperback) | ISBN 9780802498045 (ebook)
Subjects: LCSH: Motherhood--Religious aspects--Christianity. |
   Mothers--Religious life.
Classification: LCC BV4529.18 .C66 2020 (print) | LCC BV4529.18 (ebook) |
   DDC 248.8/431--dc23
LC record available at https://lccn.loc.gov/2020015685
LC ebook record available at https://lccn.loc.gov/2020015686

Originally delivered by fleets of horse-drawn wagons, the affordable paperbacks from D. L. Moody's publishing house resourced the church and served everyday people. Now, after more than 125 years of publishing and ministry, Moody Publishers' mission remains the same—even if our delivery systems have changed a bit. For more information on other books (and resources) created from a biblical perspective, go to: www.moodypublishers.com or write to:

Moody Publishers
820 N. LaSalle Boulevard
Chicago, IL 60610

1 3 5 7 9 10 8 6 4 2

Printed in the United States of America

To Abbey, Caroline, and Lauren,
For refusing to let me give up

CONTENTS

I f you spend ten minutes on social media, you will hear a bunch of different messages about being a Christian mother and wife. Most of them are filled with general platitudes about "being enough," "finding time for you," "being the best mom ever," "being true to yourself," and on and on these platitudes go. When I read them at first, I feel a hint of inspiration, but then immediately following that I feel the suffocation of knowing I won't be able to pull it off. While these inspirational quotes may seem harmless, they take root in our hearts and they turn from inspiration into rules that I feel I must live by in order to live my best life. They sound right in the moment but are actually a deadly poison.

Once I have decided that this or that rule is the remedy for my family, I see how demanding these rules are and how they bring little change and lots of heartache. I put my hope in my ability to make everything better, and I forget my Savior who already came to make everything better for me and died in my place. I see that I am putting my hope and trust in these rules when I am proud and demand of those around me: *"You see how hard I am working? You should work this hard too!"* Or when I am depressed, it's *"I will never measure up to that mom or that wife. I am not even going to try."* I know this in my heart, and yet still I am so drawn to finding the right formula or saying the right words to save myself and my family that I continue to go back to things I can do to fix it all.

I've been a parent for twenty-plus years, and if I have learned one thing it's that I am desperate for help outside of myself. I can't be all the things I should be. I can't do all the things I should do. I need a Rescuer. I need a Savior. I need a place where I can rest and find peace. I have also seen how drawn to these "inspirational" rules I am. I fear you might be drawn to these rules as well. We need help to fight against the insipid lies that draw our hearts. Dear sister, the help you need is in your hands.

Motherhood Without All the Rules: Trading Stressful Standards for Gospel Truths has done the hard work of fighting these lies for you. Maggie is a delight. Her writing is winsome and humorous and yet honest and hope-giving. Even though I haven't met her in person, I felt as though I was sitting with a friend who was helping me in a moment of crisis. As I read this book, I wished that she had written it fifteen years ago so that I could have avoided a lot of pain and confusion. But goodness, I am so grateful that you have it now. This book will shine the light of the gospel into all the dark corners where lies or half-truths have been hiding. I walked away from this book convinced that the gospel—the good news of Jesus Christ's life, death, and resurrection—really does have everything I need.

Maggie encouraged my heart in ways I didn't even know needed it. I found myself overwhelmed by the goodness of Jesus and the work that He has done. I found myself wondering at the goodness of our God. Beloved, this is what we need. We need Jesus. We need to know more of Him. We need to be utterly convinced that we are loved, seen, and known. This is our only hope. This book gives hope in large doses. As you read this book, ask the Holy Spirit to show you where you have believed in a false gospel or given yourself to a false Savior, and then repent and return to our true Savior. He is the lover of our souls.

JESSICA THOMPSON

Coauthor of *Give Them Grace*

DEAR STRESSED-OUT MOM

I have a confession: I wish I was better—a better mom, a better wife, a better friend, a better Christian. I wish I was better at reading my Bible, disciplining my kids with grace, and keeping my house clean. I don't have to be perfect, but I always wish I was a little bit better. It's really hard to live in the already-but-not-yet kingdom of God. One aspect of this "already but not yet" looks like this: if you are in Christ, you are declared righteous, but you aren't yet made perfect.

If anyone should know how to live in grace, it's me. I literally wrote a book on it. Four years ago, I discovered hope for the weakness I was struggling against in motherhood when I read 2 Corinthians 12:9–10:

> But he said to me, "My grace is sufficient for you, for my power is made perfect in weakness." Therefore I will boast all the more gladly of my weaknesses, so that the power of Christ may rest upon me. For the sake of Christ, then, I am content with weaknesses, insults, hardships, persecutions, and calamities. For when I am weak, then I am strong.

I shared in my first book, *Unsupermommy: Release Expectations, Embrace Imperfection, and Connect to God's Superpower*, how I learned to walk minute-by-minute in the thick of my helplessness but pleading for God's power to fill me up and equip me to follow His plan for my circumstances. As I met God in all my broken, insufficient places, I grew closer to Him than I ever thought possible. Those were terrifying, overwhelming, amazing years. It was a season of sanctification like nothing I had ever known before, and possibly like nothing I will experience again.

Two and a half years later, I emerged from the fog. I started to get sleep at night again. My boys began to play with each other instead of constantly needing my focused attention. They began to spend time at a glorious institution called "preschool." I started to drink my tea while it was still warm. I rediscovered the glories of morning quiet time that was often actually quiet. Life simply grew easier, and I started to grow easy with living by my own strength again.

Now that motherhood felt more manageable, I wanted to get my chance to be the good mom. The one who did everything the "right way"—*the godly way*. I considered some godly women whose motherhood I had admired as a child. It seemed like they were always busy with the work of the home—dust-free coffee tables, Crock-Pot meals, and balancing checkbooks. Then I thought about some of my peers whose motherhood and walk with God I admire now. They also work hard, but it's often balancing the needs of their children with the demands of a career and the care of their home. I wanted to be like all the moms I admired rolled into one—a hefty task!

And I didn't just want to be like them in action, I wanted to be like them in spirit too. The moms I admired managed to do so much while offering their children grace, love, and acceptance— at least that's how it looked from the outside. So, I added another thing to my list: be a mom filled with the fruit of the Spirit—love, joy, peace, patience, kindness, goodness, faithfulness, gentleness, and self-control (Gal. 5:22–23). One by one I picked up the chains I had dropped to the floor during that fiery season of toddlers and babies and slung them back over my shoulder. Ironically, in an effort to achieve godly obedience, I stopped depending on God.

I was working out my own salvation—trying to sanctify myself—with my own teeth-grinding grit instead of relying on an active relationship with God. I had begun to adopt society's system of standards to live out godly motherhood instead of doing the hard and holy work of walking with God. No wonder it wasn't working. I couldn't *exhibit* the fruit of the Spirit in relating to my children without being *in* the Spirit. I can't demonstrate the gospel to my children when I am not living in it myself.

In this information age, we are bombarded with ideas on how to be good moms. From social media to the latest research, everyone has opinions on how you should parent your children and even who you should become as a person. Inspirational quotes fill Instagram and Pinterest, touting ideals like *you just do you!* or *you're a good mom!* as pathways to freedom. These seem valuable at a glance, but you'll soon find these standards come with their own burdens. Because the world's standards and our own legalistic rules always fall short of the gospel, keeping them is stressful. "For freedom Christ has set us free; stand firm therefore, and do not submit again to a yoke of slavery" (Gal. 5:1). Jesus did not die so we could try to live up to the ideals of the world using their rules for moms. Jesus died that we might discover freedom in walking by the Spirit.

I talk to my boys a lot about following God's good plan for their lives instead of the path of the world. We talk about it a lot because I struggle with it a lot. I'm quick to start building my "kingdom of mom" according to my plan in an effort to make motherhood easier or to bring myself praise. I do this instead of embracing God's good plan of servanthood and by following the path of Jesus, the servant King.

If you want to become a better representative of the gospel to your children, you must grow in knowledge and relationship with God. My goal in writing this book is to help you grow in godliness by first helping you better understand *who* God is and *how* that impacts your motherhood. God, at His most fundamental, is a Trinitarian God—Father, Son, and Holy Spirit. Some of God's Trinitarian nature is an unfathomable mystery, but there is plenty you can understand if you study the Bible—especially the New Testament.

Paul describes the Trinity in his final greeting to the Corinthian church in 2 Corinthians 13:14: "The grace of the Lord Jesus Christ and the love of God and the fellowship of the Holy Spirit be with you all." Knowing your God of love, grace, and fellowship better will transform your motherhood from self-focused to God-glorifying.

Each of the following chapters in this book will look at one of the world's **stressful standards** for building a kingdom of mom, consider how that rule distorts our thinking, and offer a **gospel truth** about God's love, grace, and fellowship that will transform our hearts. Each chapter will end with a practical section that gives you steps for growing a **practice of holiness** by looking at one of the virtues described in 2 Peter 1:5–7. The ultimate goal isn't holiness itself. My prayer is that these practical tools for growing in holiness will be a means for you to grow nearer to our holy God.

Because you live as already saved and redeemed, but not yet holy, perfect, and sanctified, following God's best way will always be a fight to choose the gospel over the false hope the world offers in its system of rules for mothers. But fight on! This book is meant to help you in the battle. It really is hard to live in the already-but-not-yet, but—praise God!—one day, when you are taken to heaven or Jesus comes again, you will no longer have to. Therein lies your hope for today. You no longer need to focus on building up your own kingdom because your future is secure in God's kingdom. You can run hard after holiness while maintaining freedom in Christ.

CHAPTER 1

BUILDING A KINGDOM OF MOM

S hortly after I found out I was pregnant with my third son, a grandma at church pulled me aside and whispered conspiratorially: "Now you get to be queen." At the time, I was confused. Would I not have been queen if I had a daughter? Was the goal of motherhood to be the queen?

A few years later I caught myself saying to my son, "I'm not your servant." It's a common enough saying, a quick retort to throw back at our kids when their needs become ridiculous, when they're avoiding independence, or when they expect far more than we could possibly give them. But it reflected something deeper going on in my heart. I didn't want to be the servant; I wanted to be the sovereign.[1]

Mom, a title just above queen.
Every mom is a queen.
Thou shalt not try me. Mom 24:7

Cutesy sayings like these are all over Pinterest, printed on t-shirts for sale through Instagram ads, and painted on little wooden blocks at boutiques. Maybe you'd never buy one, but the idea of being a queen in charge of her world is definitely appealing. The world tells you to establish your own truth and prove yourself by your own power. If you are the ultimate authority, then your whole family benefits when you focus on meeting your needs first. You make the rules according to your opinions because mom knows best. Your children and husband should bow to your authority—why? *Because I'm the queen, that's why.*

The world invites you to take the best seat in the house. From where you sit on your throne, you can control nearly every detail of family life. You're the queen. You can govern your home, guarding your kingdom from such unspeakable disasters as too much television and unmade beds. Your children live under your ever-changing emotions and your constant stream of instructions. Your husband picks up your honey-do list and bends his knees to your meal plans. You create lists and rules, then manage your world to make them succeed. In short, you rule. Because everyone knows *if mom's not happy, no one is.*

Building your kingdom looks like freedom but quickly becomes a burden. Who can keep up with everything the world expects a mom to be? Who can bear the weight of being the one in control of your family's future? Who can manage a household, a job, and relationships with their children and still have time for self-care? As you build your kingdom according to the world, its rules for freedom become stressful standards that no one can attain.

With sovereignty comes great responsibility; the decisions of motherhood are endless and their weight feels astronomical. One wrong move and your kids will need hours of therapy to recover and live as normal human beings. The world pretends like it's all your personal choice, but one slip-up, and you're labeled a bad mom. Bad moms not only ruin their kids, but they have zero value as a person. Mess up and you may lose everything—your self-worth, your social standing, and your identity.

Of course, much of the pressure comes from the nearly constant influx of messages from the internet. The ever-changing expectations voiced by an endless stream of "experts" (and the momfluencer with 12K followers and the gingham filter for that perfect orange-y skin glow) makes it impossible to feel like you're succeeding at motherhood.

A recent study by Zero to Three, a nonprofit that supports early childhood development, found that 90 percent of moms feel judged and 46 percent feel like they're being judged almost all the time.[2] With the pressure of so many opinions, many moms choose to follow the rules simply to avoid censure.

I've bowed to rules I didn't feel conviction on more times than I realize. For years I bought my children organic snacks to eat when we were out in public and fed them the regular ones when we were at home. I felt no personal conviction on the organic/ non-organic debate but was careful to stick to organic for park time and playdates to avoid the judgment of others. Remembering to use organic at the right times wasn't easy, and as my children grew older, I grew less concerned about the opinions of others, so I sometimes forgot to stock the organic snacks. One day, as I packed my son's little fishies for lunch, I realized that because I was free from condemnation in Christ, I no longer needed to be a slave to what other people thought about my food choices.

But there is no freedom for a mom pulling the one-ton burden of her own kingdom around. God created us to work for His kingdom, not to build our own. We'd rather rule as sovereign in our little kingdom than submit to our sovereign God. We choose to follow the stressful standards of the world instead of experiencing the joy of living under God's righteous path. We prefer to maintain our role as the ultimate authority than to experience perfect parental love as a child of God. We like to work by our own insufficient power instead of living in reliant relationship with our Savior. We'd rather fix ourselves than respond to the Holy Spirit with true repentance.

We choose to follow the stressful standards of the world instead of experiencing the joy of following God's righteous path.

GRACE ISN'T EASY

God's path may be the best, but it certainly isn't the easiest. After coming out of the harrowing stage of my children's toddler years, I found myself slipping back into rule-keeping. I had emerged from the constant bombardment of needy children and life felt easier. I grew comfortable with my role as a mom and started choosing the path of least resistance: legalism. On the surface, grace seems easier than legalism. Grace is a free gift, after all, and receiving gifts isn't supposed to require any effort. But I've found accepting grace requires humility, and my prideful heart isn't always willing to take the hit.

My friend Jenna recently shared a story with me of unexpected and uncomfortable grace. While on vacation in small-town northern Minnesota, Jenna's parents (praise God for grandparents!) graciously sent Jenna and her husband on a breakfast date to a hidden gem hole-in-the-wall. As they dug into their greasy, fried breakfast treats, Jenna grew nervous. This diner was exactly the sort of place that proudly refuses to get with the times and take a credit card. When they confirmed with the waitress, their breakfast date became as uncomfortable as their creased red vinyl booth.

They had plenty of money to pay for this meal, but no way to access it. Venmo and PayPal couldn't help them here. Eating in a restaurant is supposed to be an equal transaction—you receive food and service and the restaurant receives your money. Instead of the balanced transaction they were expecting as they drove through the dense pine forests of northern Minnesota that morning, the waitress offered them grace. She told them to consider their meal paid in full.

Because of our prideful "do it yourself" mentality, we expect and find comfort in equal transactions. We don't like unpaid bills, favors from friends, and gifts we receive for no reason. Our pride wars against the imbalance of our relationship with a holy God. We owed a debt to God, and He paid it for us. Our sin on His perfect shoulders. Our weakness covered by His strength. Our failings redeemed by His amazing grace. We see the depths of the imbalance, and instead of accepting it and responding with a life full of worship, it becomes a problem for our pride. We long to repay God for the debt of our salvation but feel the weight of our inability, so we strive desperately to achieve balance through our good works. We know we must offer up acts of great importance if we will have any chance to even the scale.

Doing motherhood "right"—whatever that looks like to you based on your background or the research you have studied or the kind of family you want to build—seems like the easiest way to repay our debt. Motherhood is hard work, full of physical, emotional, mental, and spiritual effort and weighty with importance. Christian circles mistakenly call it our highest calling as women.[3] With this overemphasis on motherhood, it becomes tempting to elevate our work as moms to something weighty enough to reimburse God for the gift of salvation rather than live with the discomfort of our own inability to be holy.

Titus 2:11–14 tells us how to do life—and motherhood—right:

> For the grace of God has appeared, bringing salvation for all people, training us to renounce ungodliness and worldly passions, and to live self-controlled, upright, and godly lives in the present age, waiting for our blessed hope, the appearing of the glory of our great God and Savior Jesus Christ, who gave himself for us to redeem us from all lawlessness and to purify for himself a people for his own possession who are zealous for good works.

We can, of course, do good works with the wrong motivation—hoping to repay our salvation or give ourselves the glory. Instead, Titus tells us that God's grace sanctifies us as we fix our eyes on a greater hope—the "appearing of the glory of our great God and Savior Jesus Christ" (2:13). God did not save us to make us perfect rule keepers who no longer need Him. Instead, salvation allows us to live in reliant relationship with a holy God. Do not stop working hard at motherhood—on the contrary, Titus says to be "zealous for good works" (2:14)—but be constant in prayer that God transforms your motives from your own glory to a deeper relationship with your glorious God.

RELATIONSHIP OVER RULES

This kind of dependence on God produces the growth I really long for in this season of motherhood. I want to be a holy mom who leads her kids to the cross in both word and deed. Being a good rule follower isn't going to cut it. If I want to walk in holy motherhood, I must foster *an active reliance upon an intimate relationship with God.*

An intimate relationship begins with desire. Words like intimate and desire can make Christian women a little uncomfortable. If you've grown up in the church, you were taught that intimacy and desire were reserved for marriage, but we've gotten that backward. They aren't words relegated to the bedroom but meant to bring us to the throne room.

Remember when you had a DTR (defining the relationship) talk with that cute boy, committed to officially dating, and wanted to be together every waking moment? Or when you first met your BFF and you planned the next semester's class schedule so you could take all your gen eds together? Or when your baby first arrived and all she wanted was to be held and fed 24/7?

All our deepest human relationships begin with some sort of longing, but eventually there are seasons when that emotion is gone, and we must choose to work at nurturing the relationship despite how we feel.

Don't feel ashamed if your immediate reaction is that you rarely feel desire for God. I certainly go through seasons where I struggle to long after God in the midst of daily life. I know *what I want to want*, but my desire is lackluster. These are usually times when my gaze has been turned inward to my own needs or outward to a blessing I long for.

Every time I take my kids to Target, they plead for a trip down the toy aisle. They promise me that they just want to look, but they always end up begging for something. They will forget about most of these toys between the aisle and the checkout, but for one moment, they want them with all their heart. We shake our heads at a child's headstrong yearning, but the same is true for us: we hunger after the shiny new toy instead of enjoying the blessings we already have.

Our human tendency will always be to desire what looks valuable, exciting, and new. God is all these things, but the world is full of what will constantly entice us to turn our head. So we must diligently set the things of God before us. We need verse cards at the kitchen sink. We need worship music blaring. We need Sunday sermons and midweek Bible study. We need theologically rich podcasts in our ears as we fold laundry. We need Bibles lying open on kitchen counters until we can no longer walk past them. We must set God right in front of our face, because when we truly see God, we recognize that He is infinitely desirable.

An intimate relationship with God begins with desire but continues with knowledge. I was not a girl who developed crushes on boys very often. I had two older brothers, and my house was always filled with their friends. I knew too much about what boys were really like to be easily entranced. In high school I finally started liking boys. The initial feeling was great. That sweet rolling in my stomach when he smiled in my direction. My friends and I called it "the electric bowling ball," but you probably know it as butterflies. But the initial desire always faded as I learned more about the boy, at least until I met one very TDH (tall, dark, and handsome) boy halfway through my senior year of high school . . . that's another story for another time.

Knowing God is the opposite of all our teenage crushes. Both relationships begin with desire, but in our relationship with God the more we know about Him, the more our desire for Him grows instead of waning. Knowledge and desire are the friction and spark working together to build a burning, intimate relationship with God. If we want to experience God's nearness, we must learn more about Him through studying the Bible and identifying His faithfulness in our lives.

My husband and I have been studying up on new vehicles to find the perfect one for me. After researching several choices, we think we've found "the one," but for now we're saving our nickels and waiting until our boys are just a little older (and less likely to stain or maim that beautiful leather upholstery I'm hoping for). I'm usually terrible at identifying the make and model (don't ask me to define those terms), but now that I've found the vehicle I want, I see it everywhere. My eye is drawn to it on the freeway, the carpool line, and the Target parking lot. I've spent time studying this car, and it's lead to admiration and happiness when I see it.

In the same way, if you study the lives of Abraham and Sarah, for example, and you identify how God was faithful to them even when they were faithless, the Holy Spirit will give you eyes to see where God is being faithful to you despite your unfaithfulness. You will more quickly come to God in confession and prayer because you know how He forgives and provides. Knowing God breeds intimacy with Him because He is a God who has always been intimately involved in the lives of His people.

An active reliance on an intimate relationship with God means that we admit we aren't strong enough to bear the weight of all the rules we take on. As spoken-word artist and author Jackie Hill Perry reminds us, "The reason any Christian is still a Christian is because Christ is keeping them. Don't be so haughty as to think that you still love God because you that type."[4] After we pass through a season of survival where it is abundantly clear we are being kept by God, we cannot walk right back into living by our own strength. The countercultural truth of the gospel is the only path to the fruitfulness we are seeking.

Author Hannah Anderson explains this kind of path: "God responds to humility. He exalts those who humble themselves. This is the governing dynamic in God's upside-down kingdom: You go down in order to go up."[5] When we find ourselves living by our own power, we must confess our sin of pride and self-sufficiency and pursue active reliance on God through prayer. Then the power of sin is broken, and our good works are transformed from an avenue for self-salvation into a path of fruitful obedience.

GROWING IN GODLINESS

Walking in intimacy with God takes practice before it becomes our default. My sons started tae kwon do last month, and shortly after they started, my youngest stopped. He refused to practice unless I was with him, so I am now a proud white belt tae kwon do student (I know, you're jealous). As we learn our moves, the instructor is always trying to shift our thinking. He shouts sayings like, "Practice makes . . ." and inevitably we all respond "perfect!" But he reminds us that perfection is impossible. Instead, he teaches us to respond, "Practice makes . . . habits!"

This is true not only of tae kwon do, but also of our ability to walk in intimacy with God. When we feel the lure to measure ourselves as mothers by the world's standards, we must practice the way of our God. As we practice learning to recognize God's work in our lives because we know how He works in the Bible, the Holy Spirit transforms our hearts to long after God more than our instinctual desires for comfort and glory. Practice does not only create habits; it is part of growing in holiness.

The world tells us that moms should practice gentle responses, yoga, internet research, self-care, and so much more. These are all good things, but they will not shape us into holy moms. Instead we must practice holiness, by the guidance of God's Word and the in-working of the Holy Spirit. One of the most encouraging verses I have clung to in motherhood is 2 Peter 1:3, "His divine power has granted to us all things that pertain to life and godliness, through the knowledge of him who called us to his own glory and excellence." What an essential promise for moms! God has given to us all we need to do life and do it with godliness through knowing Him.

Peter is offering us a heavy helping of grace, but the following verses turn toward our sanctification. The paragraph continues with a list of virtues to add to our faith in Christ.

> For this reason, *make every effort* to supplement your **faith** with virtue, and **virtue** with knowledge, and **knowledge** with self-control, and **self-control** with steadfastness, and **steadfastness** with godliness, and **godliness** with brotherly affection, and **brotherly affection** with **love**." (2 Peter 1:5–7)

Because God gives us all the things we need for life and godliness, we are able to make every effort to grow in holiness by adopting practices that create space for those virtues to flourish in our lives through the work of the Holy Spirit. Jackie Hill Perry says, "Being kept by God does not mean that you be lazy about the practice of sanctification."[6] So we don't do "let go and let God"; instead, we say that *all things, including my hard mom work, are "from Him and through Him and to Him"* (Rom. 11:36).

We pursue holiness by following God's good plan for our lives presented in the commands of Scripture. Holiness produces both transformation and fruit. "For if these qualities are yours and are increasing, they keep you from being ineffective or unfruitful in the knowledge of our Lord Jesus Christ" (2 Peter 1:8). The last thing I want to be as a mom is an ineffective and unfruitful sovereign of my own kingdom. Grace is both the beginning of our salvation story and the ending. It permeates the middle portion and empowers our work for God's kingdom, but we cannot expect a harvest of righteousness without hard work. Paul says, "Not that I have already obtained this or am already perfect, but I press on to make it my own, because Christ Jesus made me his own" (Phil. 3:12).

What is the point of all this pressing on? Is it to meet the world's standards for good motherhood? Is it to achieve the esteem of our friends? Is it for children that they will one day know God themselves? No, "I press on toward the goal for the prize of the upward call of God in Christ Jesus" (Phil. 3:14). The prize isn't the admiration of the world or the members of your small group. The prize isn't Christian children. The prize isn't perfect motherhood. The prize is a deeper relationship with God on earth, until one day we experience the glory of perfect fellowship with Him in heaven.

Dear Mom Burdened by Building Her Own Kingdom,

God will not allow you to continue running hard after your own kingdom. Through His work in your heart, you will be constantly reminded that only the work of the cross can produce righteousness in our motherhood. Only when you stop relying on the rules of your self-made kingdom and start relying on your relationship with God will you experience freedom while working hard for God's glory. Then by the will of God the Father and the work of Jesus Christ, the Holy Spirit will move in your heart to produce the valuable fruit that is the foundation of godly motherhood.

CHAPTER 2

STRESSFUL STANDARD:

Everything depends on you

GOSPEL TRUTH:

God is the best parent

The first night in the hospital after the birth of my first son was one of the longest nights of my life. Every fifteen minutes or so I was wakened by the unsettling sound of his choking and coughing, as he hacked up amniotic fluid. The nurses assured me this was normal, but I was scared. They gave me a blue bulb syringe (those awful snot suckers) to clear the fluid from his mouth and left me to my own devices. I stared down into his wide eyes and realized for the first time: *I am responsible for keeping another person alive.* With that one thought I picked up my motherhood burden, fastened on my crown, and identified myself as the sovereign over my little person's life.

I had only been a mom for a few hours, but the kingdom of mom was already written in the depths of my heart in this one stressful standard: **everything depends on you**. It's a burden that moms often shoulder with pride. We wear it like a badge: *it is almost impossible, but I keep these kids alive.* In the beginning, it feels overwhelming, but as children grow, we begin to enjoy meeting all their needs. We relish those times when our big kids still need an extra bedtime snuggle to fall asleep the night before a math test. They are our needy subjects, and we are their queens.

As queen, I expect to be in control, but there's nothing like our annual trip to the local indoor water park to make me feel like my grasp is tenuous. Last year, this quick break from the cold (hello 85-degree indoor temps!) was one of the hardest eighteen hours of my life. Picture this: three clumsy boys running full-speed around a large playground being frequently doused with water, a water-slide too fast for mom but apparently just the right speed for two ambitious sons ages four and six, a lazy river with an unexpectedly hardworking current and a three-year-old insistent upon swimming without any help. To top it all off, that turbulent river led to the most terrifying feature of all: the mighty wave pool.

To a child, this place is heaven. To a mom, it is the stuff of nightmares. I felt like I was sending my kids over Niagara Falls in a barrel. In a one-night stay, we spent nine hours in the water park. My kids aren't the kind to roll up in a towel, eat snacks, and watch the other kids. They go-go-go and leave kicking and screaming when you force them to stop.

By three p.m. on our second day, I was ready to throw in the figurative and literal towel. It wasn't just the physical exhaustion. It was the mental fatigue of carefully monitoring every movement my three boys made for six hours in a row while trying to keep myself afloat. My boys still had a few hours in them, but I was so done with water that I was practically pickled. I was suffering from more than a weary body; I was undone by vigilance. Because I believed that everything depended on me, tragedy could strike if I let my guard down for even a moment. I thought that I was the only thing that stood between those raging waters and the strong lungs of my little boys.

As our children grow older, we learn that when the world says that *everything* depends on us, it means a lot more than keeping our kids alive. We are given the responsibility for not only keeping our children safe but also making sure they are also healthy *and* happy. These goals become the driving force behind our decision making. When we consider what to feed our children—Should we be sugar free? Organic? Non-GMO? Local? Unprocessed? Gluten free or dairy free?—we are attempting to control their health. As we consider their physical surroundings—Whose house can they play at? What websites can they visit? Will they attend sleepovers?—we are focused on their physical safety. When we consider how they will spend their time—What school should they attend? What extracurricular activities will they join?—we are looking to establish both their current and future happiness by setting them up to be successful.

Unfortunately, we're making our decisions based on the wrong premise. We're starting with the belief the world has ingrained into moms: that we are fully responsible for the health, safety, and happiness of our children, and it all depends on the decisions we make. When connected to this purpose, each small decision becomes as weighty as all the water in that vicious wave pool.

IF MOM IS RESPONSIBLE, MOM RULES

The biggest problem with this rule is that it sets you up as sovereign. You must be constantly on high alert to save your kids from unforeseen consequences. If your kids don't grow into healthy and happy adults, it is entirely your fault. When everything depends on you, you are responsible for each unfortunate circumstance or painful outcome.

If you believe this lie, you will hover over your children in an attempt to spare them from every pain. It's not surprising that this rule would produce a generation of helicopter parents. How can you possibly protect them from *everything* if you don't hover? Parents have become overly cautious, holding their kids back from what they should be learning to do independently in the name of safety. So, we take our children to the emergency room over minor bumps and bruises, fear public places during flu season, stop kids from climbing trees and skipping rocks. All our safety concerns have become more of a hindrance than a help.

When the responsibility for your children's actions rests on your shoulders, then naturally you must be the one to save your kids from the consequences of their own actions. It is your responsibility to send pleading emails to teachers when your kids misbehave in school. You hold back on discipline because you fear the tears welling up in their eyes and the emotional damage that may result. You believe that if you just found a new parenting technique, you'd be able to solve the problem of your kids' disobedient behavior. You bear the weight of responsibility for their actions instead of acknowledging their own sinful nature. If you believe the behavior issue is all your fault, it only makes sense to lighten the burden or bear the consequences.

If everything depends on you, then you must remain in control. This stressful standard says that you know what is best for their life, so you must always be in charge of the circumstances that surround your children. If you don't like the way a teacher or a coach is treating them, you remove them from the school or team. When your husband has different plans for your child's growth, you shut him down or "forget" to implement his ideas. Because the weight of your child's future sits on your shoulders, it becomes *absolutely essential* for you to remain in control.

THE LOVE OF A PERFECT FATHER

When I tell my oldest son that I love him, he often responds, "I love you more!" But I know there's no possible way he could love me more. I am the parent; he is the child. The love between us originated with me before he even had the ability to love. One day, Lord willing, he will have his own children and then he will understand that a child's love is only a shadow of a parent's love.

Your love for your children compels you to meet their needs, choose the best path for them even if it is a hard one, delight in them, and teach them the values you deem important. Yet, your love is still imperfect. There are days when your love for your kids isn't enough to keep you from yelling, help you let go of your to-do list to spend time interacting with them, or put their needs before your own. There are days when the requirements of motherhood feel like more than your love can give.

Even when equipped with one of the deepest kinds of human love—the love of a mother for a child—you always fall short of perfect love. You put your desires first. You expect your children to fill a void for love and acceptance in your life. You take the easy route when the hard one is the best for your children in the long run.

Even at its very best, the love of a mom for a child is a shadow of the perfect love of God. His love defies all human logic. It is completely sacrificial (Rom. 8:32). It meets all your needs—even the ones you cannot identify (Phil. 4:19). It shelters you during life's hardest seasons and only allows those seasons when they are for your good (Rom. 8:28). It satisfies your deepest longings for comfort and happiness (Ps. 145:16–19). God's love is perfectly parental.

When you know the love of a God who is your perfect parent, it is easier to entrust your children to Him. Instead of bearing the chains of everything depending on you, find freedom in trusting God to be the best parent to your child. It is God's job to keep your kids safe from physical pain, meet their emotional needs, save them from their sin, and plan the steps of their lives. When you let God be the best parent, you no longer stand in God's place in their lives. If you step back from the pressure of meeting all their needs, the Holy Spirit will be waiting to reveal God to you and to your children as you walk together through the demands and disappointments of this life.

GOD'S GOT YOUR KIDS

We just returned home from this year's annual trip to the water park and everything was different. My boys are a year older. They swim better. They are more responsible. These small changes were helpful, but what really transformed the tenor of our staycation was the change that happened in my heart. This year I remembered that the safety, health, and happiness of my children at that water park did not solely depend on me. They have a heavenly Father who cares for them perfectly and knows the course of their too-quick steps on the slippery water park floor.

This was true even when, for a moment, my youngest son ended up in over his head without a life jacket. He had just completed a rope course across one pool with much assistance from his dad. Not realizing how deep the water was or remembering that he had removed his life jacket, he immediately jumped into a large neighboring pool. My heart rammed up into my throat as I ran from the ropes course pool to where he popped to the surface only to bob under again. The terror in his eyes was mirrored in my own as I struggled to reach him. I held out my hand and he just missed it before bobbing below again. I would not leave it up to him to grab hold of me again. I reached below the surface, found the hood of his swim shirt, and hauled him up to safety.

He was terrified and a bit embarrassed. I wrapped him in a towel and hoisted his big body onto my lap, but I didn't tell him "Mom's got you," because I didn't. Instead of pointing him to the safety of my arms, I told my little guy what I knew to be true: "Sweet boy, God was watching over you. He told Mom to look up. He made her feet fast and sure as she hustled over to you. He is your heavenly Father, and He has always got you." This was the truth, because my vigilance often falls short. I could have been absorbed in my book in that moment instead of watching him make that disastrous mistake. No matter how vigilant I try to be, I'm not always watching, and I can't always keep my kids safe. God watches over their comings and goings (Ps. 121:8), and though injuries and loss still happen, they occur only within the sovereign will of our loving heavenly Father.

This is a blessing because the hard places you would try to avoid are opportunities for God to reveal Himself to your children as their heavenly Father. When you allow them to fall down or make mistakes or stew in their own foolishness, they may experience more physical or emotional pain, but they will also experience God's comfort firsthand. The psalms are a testimony to the vibrant and trusting relationship David had with God. Because he experienced God's deliverance from a young age, he clung to God as his refuge throughout his life. If you don't allow your kids to know God's deliverance firsthand, they will not develop that kind of dependent and personal relationship with God.

Because God is their perfect parent, you do not need to shield your children from the consequences of their actions. It is good for children to learn the destructiveness of their own sin. Although you want to show God's grace to your children, be careful not to downplay their need for a Savior. It is so tempting to step in too soon, to remove the weight of sin from their shoulders before they experience the godly sorrow that leads to repentance (2 Cor. 7:10) because you know how painful it is to feel guilty. Instead of ignoring consequences, gently point your children to their inability to measure up. Only then can you show them Jesus' saving work on the cross and the glorious freedom and joy of a Savior who measures up for them.

The removal of all obstacles from your children's lives also hinders their ability to find contentment. In Philippians 4:11–13, Paul explains that he learned how to be content in any situation: in hunger or plenty, in being brought low or abounding, in abundance and need. He can be content in any circumstance because he has access to God's strength. How can our children experience the ministry of relying on God's strength when they've never been allowed to experience weakness or difficulty? When all they've had is abundance, abounding, and plenty, they miss the opportunity to experience God's sufficiency through hunger, lowliness, and need and discover the secret of being content in any circumstance: Jesus Himself.

If you hold too tightly to the circumstances of your kids' lives, they will miss out on the opportunity to become independent. You are trying to protect them, but God is trying to sanctify them. Trust His sovereignty over their unpleasant circumstances and fight the urge to step in when they can learn to navigate those challenges on their own. When they are under pain or pressure, have faith that the Holy Spirit will step in to reveal God to them. Allow their heavenly Father—who numbers their days, knows every hair on their heads, and cares for even insignificant sparrows—to meet them in the uncomfortable and reign sovereign over the path of their lives. Because God is the best parent, your watchful, frantic, and burdened mom heart can find rest and freedom in pointing your children to His love and care.

A Practice of Holiness: Faith

Now it's time to tie on your "white belt" and get down to the hard work of practice. Practice makes habits, and you've had a lot of time practicing with the stressful standard that everything depends on you. If you want to let go of control and your need to be needed and learn to shepherd your children to their best parent, you need to practice **faith**. You must believe that God is who He says He is, that He will do what He has promised, and that He desires to be in relationship with you. While generally the order or stages or sequence of virtues in 2 Peter 1:5–7 isn't meaningful, it is essential that faith come first. God initiates relationship with you by grace, and you respond to Him with faith. It's the simplest tenet of the Christian life, but it is so easy to overlook. Establishing this practice of holiness will counteract your tendency to trust more in yourself than in Christ.

1. Believe that God will give you the capacity to meet the needs of your children through His strength and that He will fill in the gaps where you are lacking.

How often do you think, *I don't want my kids to need anything from me right now*? The needs of your kids can become an overwhelming burden. You may grow disgruntled every time your kids ask for help or require instruction. It seems like they always need you the exact second that you want a quiet moment. Their needs feel burdensome to you when you aren't depending on the Holy Spirit who strengthens you (Eph. 3:16) to walk in a manner worthy of your calling (Eph. 4:1). Make a habit of purposefully placing the burden of their needs at the foot of the cross instead of on your insufficient shoulders by perpetual prayer. Reach out to God for strength when you are overwhelmed. Pray not only for your own sanctification in your current weakness, but also for the spiritual growth of your children.

2. Remember your true identity: chosen, accepted, forgiven, and free through the work of Christ.

When their needs become your identity, you may avoid teaching them independence or letting their needs be met by other people (like dads and grandparents and caregivers). Your success or failure to meet their needs begins to drive your emotions when it determines your value as a mom. You can no longer entrust your children to God because your motherhood feels threatened when you are physically unable to meet their needs. Your ability or inability to do that cannot change your standing before God. Instead, remember that your identity as a redeemed daughter of God is sealed, and your inheritance is guaranteed by the Holy Spirit (Eph. 1:13–14).

3. Vulnerably share your faith in God with your children.

Your job as a mom is not to meet all your kids' needs. Your job is to shepherd them to their heavenly Father. Counselor and author Paul Tripp says that our role as a parent is to be an ambassador of God in their lives. He draws a contrast between ownership parenting, "motivated and shaped by what parents want *for* their children and *from* their children" and ambassadorial parenting, which aims to represent God and His will and plan to your children.[1] Your job isn't to save your kids from hardship but to point them to their only true Savior. The best way to show your children all the promises offered to them in Christ is to openly share about some of your own struggles to believe God and how He constantly shows you His faithfulness, care, and grace.

Dear Need-Meeting Mom,

You are not defined by your ability to meet the needs of your children. They thrive when they experience the love and care of their heavenly Father. As do you. Even when you are deep in the challenges of parenting, you are never alone. God is watching over you and caring for you as you shepherd your children toward Him.

P.S.

Read Psalm 103 for more about God
as your perfect parent.

CHAPTER 3

STRESSFUL STANDARD:

You need an escape

GOSPEL TRUTH:

God supplies exactly what you need

What do we need to be happy? According to the marketing that pops up as we stream our favorite shows or scroll our social media feeds, there's no end to what the world has to offer to make our lives better. But as moms—a job that never seems to end—we hear that **what we need most is an escape**. I'm not talking about ten days alone on a deserted island (although at the end of the summer that sounds pretty great).

On the average day, our escapes look much simpler than that: five minutes that turns into forty-five scrolling Instagram, a glass of wine after bedtime or at three in the afternoon, the salty-sweet taste of chocolate from a hidden stash, a mani-pedi, a Hallmark movie binge, or an afternoon Starbucks run. My escape of choice is a few minutes shut in my home office, drinking kombucha and playing a mind-puzzle app on my phone—ah, quiet, brain-busy bliss. Sometimes these moments are simple resets, but they have the possibility to develop into an unhealthy dependence.

Motherhood is a pendulum swing. Our work vacillates between boring and monotonous (hello, washing dishes!) and overstimulating and overwhelming (like deciphering who is at fault when two kids end up in a full-out brawl on the living room floor). We can swing between these two extremes a hundred times in one day, so it's no surprise that we are often running to our nearest escape.

It feels good to get lost in these little moments: we go to girl's night to forget the child who is continually creating discipline problems at school and home, we scroll on our phones to ease the anxiety build-up of kids who won't stop arguing, or we get lost in a book to remember that we are adults even when our brains are filled with the repetitive chatter of our children. Our escapes fill the void or ease the burden for a moment and help us feel like we're in control again. But that's all they offer—one moment. As soon as it's gone, we're looking for our next fix. Our minds grow restless for the quick buzz, for the immediate opportunity to forget our woes or responsibilities. Such happiness is fleeting, but it sparks within us the hunger for more. We find ourselves constantly looking forward to the next escape—the kid-free morning, date night, or the next season of motherhood. The danger of these good things is that we are tempted to set our hope on them.

DON'T COME BETWEEN MOM AND HER ESCAPE

We've gotten one thing right—the only way to get through our day is to hope. But these simple joys are too weak to support the weight of all the hope a mom needs to beat tedium or overwork of her daily life. There is nothing inherently bad about coffee runs, reading novels, pedicures, time with girlfriends, new clothes, massages, exercising, decorating our homes, or even taking a bubble bath, but the problem is the elevation of these good things into necessities for our happiness in motherhood.

Maybe you're reading this book, and it's your escape from whatever feels particularly hard about motherhood today. Now you feel guilty because last night's dirty dishes are still in the sink and it's two in the afternoon and you're sitting on the couch reading. I am not saying that you should be in work mode all the time and never take a break. I'm pushing you (and myself!) so we rethink how much emphasis we place on these escapes or even the weeklong vacation that'll be here next month. Do they dominate our thoughts or feel like a necessity? Or is it just as simple as fifteen minutes to refresh before we head back into the grueling work of cleaning shower grout? Are we controlling these moments or are they controlling us?

Too often, we tell ourselves that we need these breaks to survive. When mom doesn't get what she says she needs, watch out! She may burst with anger if her escape is withheld, or she may hide in a closet while chaos reigns in the rest of the home in the name of meeting her own needs. When she is queen, she not only needs her escapes, she *deserves* them for all her hard work.

Self-focus never leads to satisfaction. Your favorite escape will never fill the void in your heart meant for God alone. It is the diet soda of motherhood: instead of offering satisfaction, it leaves you endlessly thirsting for more. "You need an escape" is the world's wisdom of putting your needs front and center, but the Bible tells us that true satisfaction and joy only come through Jesus. Quick fixes never make for lasting solutions. When motherhood feels like both too little and too much, your escape will only last for a moment, but the soul-care sustenance of escaping to God's care changes your heart for a lifetime.

GOD'S ABUNDANT CARE

It is readily apparent that children are not very good at identifying what they need. One of my sons is convinced that he needs an applesauce pack every time we get in the car, but I know that he's actually thirsty. I insist on the water; he insists on the applesauce but eventually changes his tune. Now he *needs* a sucker, and a new Pokémon card, and a TV show. But children are not the only ones who aren't good at identifying their true needs, which is why Paul Tripp calls *need* "the sloppiest, most all-inclusive word in the human language."[1] Most of what you may label a need is really something you want.

Needs make almost any behavior justifiable. You can be angry, withdrawn, or passive if you're not getting what you need. You can neglect the physical and emotional needs of your children when you aren't properly equipped yourself for the job. Be careful what you label a need in your own mind. It certainly is nice to have a grocery run sans kiddos, but the minute you say that you need it, it begins to control you.

So, what do you really need to be a happy mom? When you buy into the stressful standard that you need an escape, you become responsible for both correctly categorizing your needs and making sure they are met. You probably feel pretty good about your ability to anticipate needs. It's part of a mom's job description.

When we head to the family cabin for the weekend, we embark on a two-and-a-half-hour car ride that possibly turns into four or more, depending on how many Minnesotans have chosen to make that mass exodus out of the Twin Cities with us. As the mom, I am careful to anticipate the needs of my family for the trip. I pack approximately 732 snacks (in my house, full tummies equal happy kids), juice boxes and water bottles, tablets, books, toys, blankets, pillows, and one of those handy hospital barf bags. This is just what we need for the car ride—it doesn't include everything we require for the actual weekend at the lake.

How do my kids prepare to leave for the cabin? They just get in the car. They don't worry if they are equipped for the ride ahead; they trust that their mom has been faithful to consider their needs. Inevitably, one of my sons gets sleepy as we drive and complains, "I wish I had my car pillow."

My mouth turns up at the corner: I have anticipated this need. "You mean the one sitting on the luggage behind your head?" Our eyes meet across the crowded car, and we giggle together. He feels good because his need was met, and I'm happy that I was able to anticipate it. In that short connection, our relationship deepens. He is reminded that I am a safe place to put his trust.

These moments are special, but I'll admit that I grow burdened by the responsibility to anticipate everyone's needs. How sweet it is then, as a mom, to have one relationship where I am not responsible for the needs of another. If you are in Christ, the triune God adopted you into His perfect family: "See what kind of love the Father has given to us, that we should be called children of God; and so we are" (1 John 3:1). In this adoption, you receive the Holy Spirit, who teaches you to cry out to God as "Abba! Father!'" (Gal. 4:4–6).[2] Abba—Daddy—not just father, or dad, but *daddy*. Daddy is personal. Daddy is the One whose love you know through experience. You have a heavenly Father, and He knows your needs better than you ever can. He sees the whole picture of your life and is working out your past, present, and future together for your good and His glory.

Philippians 4:19 promises, "And my God will supply every need of yours according to his riches in glory in Christ Jesus." He meets your unanticipated and felt needs by the abundance of grace bought through Jesus' saving work on the cross. Right after Paul promises that God will supply our needs with Himself, Paul immediately turns to praise: "To our God and Father be glory forever and ever. Amen" (Phil. 4:20). When you expect God to meet your needs and rejoice when those expectations are met, you are participating in a glory cycle. It is by His glory that your needs are met, and the meeting of them gives you joy and brings God even more glory. When you get inside this glory cycle, you discover a firm foundation for your hope, a deeper satisfaction than the temporary buzz of an escape.

Part of your job as a mom is to not only identify the needs of your children and meet them, but to move your kids toward independence and away from their need of you. It is not so with God. As you mature in your relationship with God, you spend less time holding tightly to your personal kingdoms and more time serving in God's, where you learn to embrace your need for Him. Spiritual maturity rejects the notion that this world offers enough hope for your day and depends completely upon God's grace for all your needs.

The late missionary and author Elisabeth Elliot offers Peter's response to Christ as a model for how we can turn from the offerings of the world for escape to the better gift of God Himself:

> Throughout our earthly lives, it is always at the point of need—that moment of crisis when we cast about for some solution or answer or even some escape—that the opportunity is offered to us to *choose*. We will accept either the solutions, answers, and escapes that the world offers (and there are always plenty of those), or the radical alternative shown to the mind attuned to Christ's. The ways of the world exalt themselves against God. They sometimes look rational and appealing to the most earnest disciple, but Christ says to us then what He said to His disciples long ago, when many of them had already given up in disgust, "Do you also want to leave me?" If we answer as Peter did, "Lord, to whom shall we go? Your words are words of eternal life," our rebel thoughts are captured once more. The way of holiness is again visible. The disciple steps forward through the narrow gate.[3]

Elliot points out our two choices: the world's escapes or God Himself. It is the path of following the person of Christ that leads to holiness. The world has many appealing offerings when we find ourselves overworked or underwhelmed, but God offers all we need through a relationship with Him.

A Practice of Holiness: Self-Control

When you practice the gospel habit of self-control, you learn to use methods of self-care that lead to true rest. Self-control is not trendy or exciting. Saying no to your desire for escape is, by definition, uncomfortable, but in denying your temporary satisfaction in the escapes of this world, you will train yourself to long after true satisfaction in Christ. Self-control enables you to deny the easy escape that keeps you in control of your comfortable kingdoms and, instead, to long after an all-satisfying intimacy with God.

Because physical and spiritual renewal are interwoven, you shouldn't separate your physical care from your spiritual experience. Self-control chooses physical experiences that build your faith in God instead of your comfort. Don't overlook that self-control is a fruit of the Spirit. "We tend to think of self-control as a strictly human enterprise, but Scripture describes self-control as a product of being connected to God."[4] If you want to grow in this, you must rely on the Spirit instead of yourself. A simple prayer of "Lord, I need Your help with this" can transform a self-reliant moment into a Spirit-filled fruit. As you grow in fruitful self-control, these habits will transform your quick escapes into moments of true renewal in Christ:

1. Embrace your neediness.

Two women may perform the same acts of self-care and receive two entirely different results because one is idolizing her needs and the other is humbly accepting her physical and emotional limitations. This humble acceptance is the first step of self-control. God made you from dust. Your body and your abilities are finite. The lists you create for your days are often beyond the abilities of your human body. Quick escapes focus on what you can do to renew yourself, but soul-care turns your eyes upward for God's provision. By establishing that you can't be God, it frees you to accept your weaknesses, and then to receive His unending strength. Soul-care flows from the humble recognition that your physical body is finite and ineffectual, but God gives you supernatural grace that is everything you need for life and godliness (2 Peter 1:3).

2. Give your mind real sustenance.

To be good soul-care, your method for rest must allow you to learn more about God and draw nearer to Him. Self-care aims to give physical and psychological renewal, but soul-care accesses what your soul craves. As a mom, I often feel muddled from lack of rest, unable to understand how to practically apply wisdom to the intricate challenges of motherhood. I feel overwhelmed and unsure. These are sure signs that I am depriving my soul. When you feel the need for a quick escape, the first thing you should do is feed yourself God's Word. The Word of God and the truth of the gospel will reorient your thinking.

3. Expect your rest to change your heart.

You grow in holiness when you experience more of your heavenly Father. Yes, effective self-care provides physical rest, but it also leads to sanctification. Your regular self-care activities transform into something deeper when they are a means of opening your heart to the Holy Spirit. Pray for God to reveal Himself to you. Recognize what a gift of amazing grace it is for the stony places of your heart to be made into flesh. Confess your sins and your utter inability to do life without God. Let whatever activity you choose lead your heart to the life-giving, life-changing awesomeness of God. This is not over-spiritualization, but an effort to remind yourself that God created both mind and body, and He speaks to you not only through a set-aside quiet time, but also through your physical experiences.

Dear Unsatisfied Mom,

You cannot expect that a simple escape will satisfy your deepest longings or help you survive until the next season. Quick fixes never fix anything. May you trust God to both correctly identify and meet all your needs. Author Drew Dyck writes in his book *Your Future Self Will Thank You: Secrets to Self-Control from the Bible and Brain Science*, "Biblical self-control is about keeping our loves in the right order. In a sense, we can only do what we love. When we succumb to sin, it's because in that moment, we loved something else—pleasure, pride, comfort—more than God. We will always operate out of our loves."[5] So, when you practice self-control instead of giving in to an easy escape, you'll reorder your loves and develop your conviction that God's provision is better than all the escapes of the world.

P.S.

Read Psalm 145 to learn more
about the God who meets your needs.

CHAPTER 4

STRESSFUL STANDARD:

You deserve it

GOSPEL TRUTH:

Your loving God disciplines you

We are moms. We know about being uncomfortable. We know about surviving delayed meals, deciphering complex sibling arguments, sitting in bleachers for hours, and making complicated life decisions for other people. Motherhood isn't primarily the land of dance parties and laughing until your sides hurt. Those things happen, of course, but it is more often the land of sacrifice and heartbreaking discipline. It is the place where we juggle hundreds of responsibilities and activities and relationships that feel like they are asking for more than we can give.

No one enjoys discomfort. I personally hate it. I don't think I knew the depth of my aversion to discomfort until I became a mom. Very little about motherhood feels easy. Just as soon as you've got it figured out and decide you can sit back and let life slip by, your season changes as your children grow and change and you must figure out what intentional motherhood looks like all over again. This is a tough job, whether you're a mom of one or seven, single or married, working or at home—motherhood is hard, so when a mom gets what she's been longing for, the world assures her *you deserve it!*

THE WRONG KIND OF TROPHY

When we experience challenge, the world tells us that we deserve a corresponding comfort or blessing to bring our life back into balance. One of my dear friends was single for over a decade past most of her peers. At thirty-seven, she finally married, ready to build the family she had longed for, but her plans were stalled by infertility. Everyone who loved her revolted. *A long season of singleness followed by infertility, Lord? It's just too much. If anyone deserves childbearing to be easy, it's her!* We needed her singleness to be balanced out by the blessing of children. Anything else seemed unjust. We thought children should be her trophy after all those hard years of faithfulness in the waiting.

I suppose this is why the Old Testament story of Hannah has always been uncomfortable for me. This dear woman is the favorite of her husband's two wives, but she has not been given children while the other wife is a fertile myrtle. On their annual trip to the temple, Hannah becomes distraught while praying for a child—it is truly the deepest desire of her heart. But while she is "pouring out [her] soul before the Lord" (1 Sam. 1:15), she offers to give any child God may bless her with back to God. So, when God gives her a son, Samuel, she brings him to the temple once he is weaned. Doesn't this feel unfair? After all her years of longing, when she finally gets a child, Hannah must honor her promise to God and give him away for temple service. It's painful to imagine the depth of that sacrifice.

So we immortalize her words on baby onesies and nursery art: "For this child I prayed, and the LORD has granted me my petition that I made to him" (1 Sam. 1:27). But the next verse is not so popular: "Therefore I have lent him to the Lord. As long as he lives, he is lent to the LORD" (1 Sam. 1:28). Why can't Hannah just keep the baby she prayed for? Why does she have to give him up? But Hannah doesn't react to the gift of her son with an "I deserve this" attitude. In humility, she recognizes that this blessing came from God, and offers it back to Him in worship. Thankfully, we get to see the rest of the story: Samuel grows up in the temple and becomes the next priest, replacing the wicked sons of Eli. And God sees Hannah's humility and worship and blesses her with three more sons and two daughters (1 Sam. 2:21).

I tried to balance the scales of painful places with a good blessing once myself. I spent my entire life looking forward to having a daughter. My mom is my best friend and my spiritual mentor, and I anticipated developing the same kind of relationship with my imagined daughter. But she never came, and boy, was the loss of that dream painful.[1] Despite the immense blessing of my three boys and the joy I was finding in being their mom, I still grieved over not having one more baby—the long-awaited daughter. While I was still deep in grief, God graciously opened the door for my family to build a house on my parents' beautiful hobby farm. It's the kind of blessing that I'm still a bit speechless over.

Many well-meaning believers who knew our story of daughter disappointment would walk into our new home on the old family farm and spout the accepted wisdom, "You deserve this." Inwardly I'd cringe; I know my sin nature well enough to know that's not true. I definitely don't *deserve* my beautiful farmhouse on my family's land. But that didn't stop me from trying to use this blessing to balance out the weight of my disappointment. I told myself, "See! God gives you good gifts! Now be happy!" It didn't work. I failed to realize that no earthly gift has the power to bring lasting contentment and satisfaction.

No matter how hard we work or how many painful circumstances we've been through in motherhood, we don't deserve any of the earthly blessings we have been given. Not only do we not deserve them, but we cannot set our hope for happiness in them. When God gives moms the discomfort of endless service to others and one of the myriad of emotional pains we experience as we watch our children walk through this broken world, earthly blessings cannot get us back into balance. God has a good purpose in allowing unbalanced scales, and His purpose will not be served by our finding comfort in this world. God allows the pain of imbalance so we will grow in maturity, finding comfort and peace in Him alone while becoming holy in the process.

THE GOODNESS OF TOUGH LOVE

So far, I've written about God's love in a way that is easy to embrace. Who wouldn't accept a God who loves us enough to bear the weight of parenting our children perfectly? Who won't follow a God who provides us with exactly what we need through His perfect wisdom? But there's another part to the story, a place where God's love isn't all sunshine and rainbows. If we are to grow in relationship with a holy God, we must also grow in holiness. We are God's children, after all, and children become like their parents.

In the age-old debate about nature or nurture, we know that it's about both. Art Van Zee—the father of my dad—left his wife and children when my dad was only five and never looked back. My dad grew up with zero nurture from his earthly father. Art moved across the country and started a new family, had another daughter who believed she was an only child most of her life. As an adult she learned about the existence of five half siblings. Our families started visiting each other, attempting to build bonds between siblings who hadn't known about each other's existence.

During one visit, my dad fell asleep on the couch in his usual napping position: arms up near his ears, elbows crooked, hands creating a soft pillow for his head. I have seen my dad sleep like that more times than I could ever count, but it startled his half-sister. She had seen their dad nap like that more times than she could recall too. My brothers and I sometimes catch ourselves in the same unusual position, and we've been delighted to see our own kids carry on this surprisingly comfortable sleeping position. My dad barely knew his father, and I never knew my grandpa, and yet, part of him lives in us, buried deep in our DNA.

But how we act is not just the sum of our DNA. I have a friend who adopted her children as embryos. Although she gave birth to them, they share no genetic connection. We have been surprised and delighted by how much those children act like their parents. I think this is because God was gracious to plant some similarities in their DNA, but mostly because they live in active, reliant relationship with their parents. Knowing their parents deeply is transforming who they are.

The same is true for us. We are post-fall humans, born sinners through the line of Adam. Yet, God sees fit through the shedding of His own blood on the cross to bring us into His family, making us new creations—creatures with new DNA. We are now His children. "See what kind of love the Father has given to us that we should be called children of God; and so we are" (1 John 3:1). As God's children, we grow to act more like our Father.

Along with our new DNA, we live under the loving nurture and discipline of God, which always produces change. God not only changed our nature when He saved us but also nurtures us to grow more Christlike as we live in intimate relationship with Him. Nurture has gentle connotations, but our growth often requires pressure and pain.

Moms know about discipline. Some days it feels like it's the only thing we do. We know that discipline is more than anger-induced punishment. We know that good discipline is about helping our children grow and mature. It includes teaching them what God's truth is instead of letting them make up their own. It means setting boundaries when the world tells our children there are no limits. It might even mean withholding good things so they might experience the best instead of treating them to everything they desire.

Moms know that the best discipline happens in moments of discomfort. When our kid fails the test, stumbles onto an inappropriate website, continues to fear the dark long after it is age-appropriate, or misses the game-winning sho

discomfort that creates opportunities for disc

Despite what the world may like us to beliey

from love (Heb. 12:5–6). The writer of Heb

word for discipline as Paul uses in 2 Timothy 3:16 when he asserts that Scripture should be used for *"teaching, for reproof, rebuking, for correction, and for training in righteousness."* This loving discipline is not punishment that forces acquiescence to your rule, but shepherding that prompts a heart work as you train your child to live the way God instructs believers to live.

As the perfect parent, God knows so much more than we do about discipline. He perfectly understands the necessity of boundaries, truth, and withholding good things for better ones. We are the children of this wise, loving, and perfect Father. Because He loves us, He allows discomfort for the goal of growth. He wants us to become what He has already declared us to be: righteous, holy, and free. Just as God our heavenly Father made the hard decision to send Jesus to die on the cross that we might be saved, He is not afraid to make hard decisions so we might mature in holiness. In God's kingdom, we don't deserve comfort and ease, and *He is actually too kind to give them to us.* When we are comfortable and capable, we rarely grow. In our discomfort, we discover the joy of completing a marathon of sacrifice and discipline instead of a vacation in the muck of our heart's earthly desires.

God's discipline is so much greater than our weak, imperfect attempts at disciplining our own children or the discipline we received from our own parents.

For they disciplined us for a short time as it seemed best to them, but he disciplines us for our good, that we may share in his holiness. For the moment all discipline seems painful rather than pleasant, but later it yields the peaceful fruit of righteousness to those who have been trained by it. (Heb. 12:10–11)

In chapter 2, I made the case for trying not to shelter and protect our children from moments of discomfort, for that may be what God intends for their growth. But now we see that it is the same for us. That as children of God, our good Father allows discomfort so we may grow in holiness and grow in nearness to Him. Yet we tend to cower from the uncomfortable as much as we can. By definition, moments of discomfort and pain aren't easy, but they yield good fruit if we see them as God's loving opportunities for growth.

KINGDOM OF LOVING DISCIPLINE

On God's good blessing of a hobby farm, we share cows and horses with my parents and raise fainting goats ourselves. (Put "fainting goats" into the YouTube search bar next time you need a good laugh.) Recently, we've had our first round of kids. That's what goat babies are called—not confusing at all, I know. These first-time mamas had no idea what was happening. They don't know they are pregnant. All they know is that it hurts. Lying down is uncomfortable. Sleeping is difficult. Life becomes increasingly painful—and for what?

They look at us with accusing eyes. They think we did this to them, and I suppose we did. But we do it because we know that a baby is the result. The mamas can't see the end, though; they are trapped in the here and now. They have to trust us because they know that we are their caretakers and we know what's best for them. We understand that all these labor pains will be worth it. After much agony, a kid comes (or two or three or even four!— I'm glad I'm not a goat). We set the baby by the new mama's face and encourage her to lick away the amniotic sac in order to bond with her kid. She looks up at us like we've grown three heads. This thing? This wet, crying, spindly thing was the purpose of all that discomfort?

It doesn't seem right, but with some prodding, they give in. They lick. They embrace what has been put before them, and somewhere in that initial cleaning and first feed, their eyes are opened. Of course, these sweet, cuddly, stumble-y little kids were worth all the pain. They have experienced the difficult process of the gift of new life, and they are changed by it. Some quiet goats become demanding mothers. Some independent goats become needy for the affection of their caretakers after giving birth. Some laid-back goats become downright territorial over their kids. As their caretakers, my husband and I know what's happening to them and the change and growth and blessing it will produce, but in the process our goats are forced to trust us.

God's uncomfortable, loving discipline is just as confusing. You may get locked forever in the process of a first-time goat mama. The typical human response to painful discipline is to either take it too lightly or become weary.

And have you forgotten the exhortation that addresses you as sons? "My son, do not regard lightly the discipline of the Lord, nor be weary when reproved by him. For the Lord disciplines the one he loves, and chastises every son whom he receives." (Heb. 12:5)

If you try to numb or avoid the uncomfortable through the escapes of this world—social media, wine, Netflix, chocolate, and so many others—you take God's discipline too lightly. In turning to these escapes, you fail to recognize that only the presence of God can sustain you in difficult circumstances.

If your response to God's discipline is complaining and questioning, you are experiencing weariness at His reproof. These responses bypass the growth opportunity God has intended for you. They make the painful circumstances even harder. Paul Tripp says you don't just suffer your circumstances, but you also suffer from how your heart responds to your circumstances.[2] When life is hard, uncomfortable, or downright painful, you may wonder why God would allow this. You might wonder why even though you work so hard and are experiencing so much pain, you don't ever receive blessings that look as good as those of the woman across the aisle at church or across the vast expanse of Instagram. You can't imagine anything good ever coming out of this experience.

Finally, after you've endured much pain and toil, God may open your eyes to His purpose. The holiness wrought through the flames of painful circumstance deepens your intimacy with your holy God. He means for you to walk in difficult circumstances knowing that the end goal is holiness (Heb. 12:10) and that His discipline will yield the "peaceful fruit of righteousness" when we respond with the willingness to be trained (Heb. 12:11). God sets the blessing before you like we set the goat kids before their moms. Like those moms, you may wonder if the fruit of holiness is actually worth the pain. Then God opens your eyes and you finally see the glory of new creation.

A Practice of Holiness: Knowing God Better

Peter includes knowledge of God in his list of virtues that will keep us from being ineffective or unfruitful (2 Peter 1:8). Identifying the kind discipline of God in simpler seasons gives you a knowledge of how God's discipline works so the correct response becomes a habit in more painful seasons of intense sanctification.

Master Raberge, our tae kwon do instructor, is a sixth-degree black belt. He often tells us the story of his recent belt-test. He didn't practice much for the test—his full-time job is teaching others how to do martial arts; why would he need extra practice? So, he knew the right moves, but he hadn't put in the extra effort to make them a habit. He failed that test even though he technically knew what to do. He put on his sparring gear and spent a month practicing with all he had. He took the test again and passed it with ease. His body knew what to do this time and could respond automatically despite the strain of the test.

In motherhood's everyday uncomfortable moments, we develop a gospel habit that accepts God's discipline as we experience the painful, next-level trials of mom life.

1. Submit something small to God's lordship.

Maybe it's letting the dishes go until morning so you can go on a bike ride with your kids after dinner. Maybe it's a break from the distractions of social media. Maybe it's saying no to another school volunteer event because you haven't had much time to spend in your Bible lately. Maybe it's skipping the afternoon coffee you swear you need to survive. Maybe it's taking a nap on Sunday instead of doing the laundry. Start simple. Submit your desire for control or perfection or comfort, and then watch how God uses that discomfort to teach you to rely on Him.

2. Note your responses to God's discipline and pray for the Holy Spirit to help you change.

In his devotional *My Utmost for His Highest*, Oswald Chambers describes how many respond to God's discipline:

> He says to you, in effect, "Don't be blind on this point any-more—you are not as far along spiritually as you thought you were. Until now I have not been able to reveal this to you, but I'm revealing it to you right now." When the Lord disciplines you like that, let Him have His way with you. Allow Him to put you into a right-standing relationship before God. "... nor be discouraged when you are rebuked by Him." We begin to pout, become irritated with God, and then say, "Oh well, I can't help it. I prayed and things didn't turn out right anyway. So I'm simply going to give up on everything." Just think what would happen if we acted like this in any other area of our lives! Am I fully prepared

to allow God to grip me by His power and do a work in me that is truly worthy of Himself? Sanctification is not my idea of what I want God to do for me— sanctification is God's idea of what He wants to do for me.[3]

Pouting denotes pride. A pouting child won't listen to reason or see the bigger picture. As a parent, you have goals for how you want your child to mature. Because these goals are beyond their understanding, they cannot fully grasp the purpose behind your decisions.

God wants to grow you through the pressures of daily life: when your son forgets his backpack at home; when your sick baby keeps you from a special lunch with a friend that you've been planning for months; or when an unexpected work issue keeps you from attending your daughter's soccer game. These small pain points are opportunities for sanctification when you learn not to give up on a holy response just because it doesn't come naturally. Through prayer, God may open your eyes to the work He wants to do in your soul in these small annoyances, further preparing you for the more strenuous moments of sanctification ahead.

3. Look forward to the joy to come.

As you experience painful circumstances, it is easy to grow disheartened. During the Last Supper, Jesus spent time preparing His disciples for the fear, confusion, and persecution they would walk through during His crucifixion, resurrection, and their sharing of the gospel and service to the early church. Life would not be easy for the disciples, but God would sanctify them through the process of trial and tribulation. Jesus reminds them to put their hope in His work of salvation: "In the world you will have tribulation. But take heart; I have overcome the world" (John 16:33). Jesus concludes their time together by praying that God keep the disciples in the faith and sanctify them through the challenges ahead. The hope of the disciples lay in Jesus' hard road to the cross and His victory over sin and death through His resurrection.

Your hope is the same. In this world, you will have troubles, but you will always have the hope of your relationship with God. It may be marred by our imperfection now, but one day you will experience unencumbered joy in His glorious presence—a gift you will never deserve.

Dear Uncomfortable Mom,

These challenging circumstances are for your good. Your heavenly Father is treating you as His child. Though this discipline feels painful now, it will produce a harvest of holiness in your life. When life isn't comfortable, you can experience the fullness of joy only possible in His presence, not because you deserve it, but because Jesus earned it.

P.S.

Read 1 John 4:7–21 and consider how
God's love transforms you.

CHAPTER 5

STRESSFUL STANDARD:
You do you

GOSPEL TRUTH:
Discover freedom through repentance

It's raining today. I'm sitting in my bedroom at the small desk from my childhood that I use as a nightstand, typing away while my two youngest boys enjoy the treat of a bath in my oversized tub. Even on this gray day, I'm distracted by the beauty outside my window. I live in an idyllic place. Our lawn ends at a gravel lane that provides access to the barn on the other side of our property. We've encroached on our neighbors a bit—our playground and garden sit on their land on the other side of the lane (nicknamed "Maggie Lane" after our neighbors' only daughter). Our neighbors' lawn ends in a large pond with a little island.

On the other side of my house, the goats are probably hiding in their red and white shed, or maybe braving the rain to fill their stomachs with the small green shoots of spring. In the next pasture, the shaggy beef cows are sunk to their knees in mud scavenging for any hint of new growth. There are open fields and treed hills and more underbrush than our goats can manage to keep in check. In a small circle of pastures surrounding a gray barn, our stocky cream-colored horses rub up against their wooden fence posts, attempting to shed their long winter coats.

I live in a picture-postcard place. You may recall from the last chapter that our next-door neighbors are actually my parents, and Maggie Lane Farm is named after me. It was cute when I was a child, but could be a bit embarrassing now that I live here as an adult. Who am I kidding? I love that I still get to live on the farm named after me.

On the days when I look out and don't just see the familiar surroundings but truly behold their beauty, I'm awestruck by the grace of it. I have earthly parents who love me well—not because of anything I am or have done, but just because I am theirs. Because they love me (and my husband and my boys), they gave us a portion of their property. As part of this gift, the boundaries of my parents' original parcel had to be redrawn. It gave me a new appreciation for the words of the psalmist, "The lines have fallen for me in pleasant places; indeed, I have a beautiful inheritance" (Ps. 16:6). I can't imagine a more beautiful earthly inheritance.

As a grace gift always does, it created an imbalance in our relationship. The first year here was an undeniable blessing, but I was also acutely aware of how much I had been given.

So, I tried to make things even. How many times would I need to pull their garbage cans up from the curb to repay them? How often should I mow their lawn? Help my dad with a farm project? Send up our dinner leftovers for their meal? I struggled to brainstorm enough acts of service to make a dent in the gift they had offered us, but I couldn't. On top of this debt, it seemed like every time I helped them, they managed to serve me back. When I missed an opportunity, I felt ashamed—would they think I was ungrateful? Would they regret offering me this gift?

Until one day, I stood outside of my parents' garage after dropping off my kids for a playdate at Grandma's so I could finally complete a project. Lost in a spiral of shame, I barely registered a flock of geese as they skimmed across the quiet pond, fragmenting the reflection of the sun into a thousand tiny pieces. A choice lay before me: work endlessly to make some small dent in what I owed or just accept this land as grace. No matter how hard I tried, I could never earn, deserve, or repay them, but there was no shame in a parent's abundant love. From the security of that love, I am freed to work out of gratefulness instead of shame. The more I consider their love for me displayed in this beautiful inheritance, the more joy I find in serving them. This is how grace defeats shame and motivates good works.

LIVING IN A KINGDOM OF SHAME

Unfortunately, motherhood is more often marked by shame than joy. We've all experienced mom-shaming in one form or another—from an in-law, another woman at a mom's group, or the random lady in the grocery store—but we often don't recognize that our primary source of shame comes from inside ourselves. Mom-shame is more of a battle in our minds than on the playground.

Counselor Ed Welch defines shame as "the deep sense that you are unacceptable because of something you did, something done to you, or something associated with you. You feel exposed and humiliated."[1] Shame isn't just about our actions, but *who we are*.[2] It's an issue of identity. Shame is a feeling. It's the knot in your stomach after you realized you didn't even hear your child's request because your phone had your focus. It's the quiet fear that one of your kids has a hard heart to the gospel no matter how many times you present it. It's the longing to believe you're a good mom even though you yelled at your kids before you'd finished your morning coffee.

It took me years to recognize the voice of my shame. I tally up the weight of my personal choices against those of other moms. I recite lists of how I messed up at motherhood in this last week or the last eight years. I stew in how I must be a disappointment to my husband and kids. I let my choices and actions dictate my identity, and I'm ashamed of the results.

Motherhood mostly happens in private—primarily in our own homes where few besides our children have the opportunity to witness both our real and supposed failures. In the unquiet recesses of my brain, I struggle with my self-worth—*Am I any good at this? Does my work have value? Do I have value?* Thoughts that would sound too extreme spoken out loud find a place to thrive and grow in the inner sanctum of a mom's mind.

There isn't a mom in this world who doesn't know she's messed some stuff up, but the world's solution is to shrug shame off by embracing our personalities: ***you just do you!*** We're told that our failures aren't really our fault, they're just who we are.

Unfortunately, this doesn't diminish shame, but cements it. The inner voice continues to taunt.

The scariest thing about inner mom-shaming? Mistaking our internal condemnation for God's voice. Shame builds a wall between us and God. We know God is holy, so we keep Him at arm's length. We hope that if He doesn't get too close, He won't see our faults. But we're right; from the moment Eve ate of the fruit, there *has* been something inherently wrong with us. We are sinners, and shame tells us that we'll never be anything but sinful failures. When the narrative stops at our sin, we must hide our shame from our holy God. Sadly, we're missing the rest of the story. We've reached the wrong conclusion. We've gotten stuck at the beginning and forgotten the rest of the gospel.

A KINGDOM OF GRACE

The good news of God's grace is more than a game changer, it's a shame changer. "Grace is the free blessing of God that flows from His heart to guilty, undeserving sinners."[3] God saves us because He chose to, not because He was under any moral obligation to do so. Humans failed, are failing, and will fail again to live up to His standard of righteousness. Susanna Wesley, mother of nineteen children including the theologians John Wesley and Charles Wesley, summarizes grace this way: "as he did not create, so neither did he redeem because he needed us; but he loved us because he loved us."[4] We do not receive grace based upon anything we do, but simply because God chose to offer it to us.

Adam and Eve broke their perfect relationship with God, but

He still sent His only Son to make an intimate relationship between God and humans possible again. His grace knows no end. Even though we will continue to sin after we've first accepted this free gift of salvation, God sent His very Spirit to help us accept His grace and equip us to grow in deeper relationship with Him. Our kind God prompts us to respond in worshipful good works.

GRACE CYCLES

If you self-reflect a little deeper than the latest personality craze, you know your need for grace. You've experienced cycles of fail, try harder, fail, try harder, fail again. Even after salvation, you may struggle with this personal responsibility, try-harder attitude toward sanctification. Now your cycle appears a little holier: pray, try, fail, repent, grow, pray, try, fail, repent, grow. The apostle Paul describes this problem in Romans 7:18–19: "For I have the desire to do what is right, but not the ability to carry it out. For I do not do the good I want, but the evil I do not want is what I keep on doing."

Could there be a more accurate description of our motherhood? You know the kind of mom you want to be, but no matter how many good books you read, goals you set, verses you tape on the window behind your kitchen sink, and internet research you do, it's hard to live up to everything you've planned. Life happens. Kids happen. Sin happens. Your motherhood doesn't occur in the perfect bubble of your imagination, but in the nitty-gritty, fallen world full of broken people.

When you feel stuck in an endless cycle of grace-work-repentance-repeat, you wonder if you'll ever attain the coveted title of "godly mom." I recently started discipling three moms of very little children. One of the first things I told them was that it is a gift for me to get to speak into their lives in a season when they will experience so much growth and sanctification. One of them responded, "It certainly doesn't feel like it, but I hope so." Sanctification is hard to identify when you're in the middle of it.

Seasons of hidden growth can be discouraging. They don't feel abundant and prosperous; they feel painful and dry. Of course, how you feel isn't always an accurate representation of what is happening. Sometimes you will feel like your feet are glued in one place on the journey toward God and godliness, but what you don't realize is that you are actually standing on one of those flat escalators you use in airport terminals. If you are in Christ, you are on a people mover of God's grace, and even when you feel stuck do not give in to despair, but continue to walk by the power of the Holy Spirit, who does not stop moving.

God uses such seasons to help us recognize your weakness that you may better receive the power of God's grace. If you are saved, God is sanctifying you (1 Cor. 6:11). In her book *Extravagant Grace*, counselor Barbara Duguid explains how God can use your failures to lead you toward greater sanctification:

> God thinks that you will actually come to know and love
> him better as a desperate and weak sinner in continual need
> of grace than you would as a triumphant Christian warrior
> who wins each and every battle against sin. This makes
> sense out of our experience as Christians. If the job of the
> Holy Spirit is to make you more humble and dependent

on Christ, more grateful for his sacrifice and more adoring of him as a wonderful Savior, then he must be doing a very, very good job even though you still sin every day.[5]

Your sin and failure are opportunities for humility, which leads to repentance. If you try walking against the momentum of God's grace, you will become exhausted by self-righteousness or wounded by painful falls into pits of sin. Repentance refocuses our hearts onto God; it turns us back in the right direction. Walking in step with the direction of God's instructions brings joy. When you follow His guidance, you experience the pleasure of walking at an outrageous speed, the joy of the wind breezing through your hair as you experience God's good plan for your life.

In that moment you don't glory in the power of your feet but the force below that propels them forward. God opens your eyes and you recognize how He's been faithful to keep you moving even when you felt like you were at a standstill.

JESUS, SHAME-BREAKER

It's a gift to realize that you can't do godly motherhood by your own power, because self-righteousness keeps you from recognizing your need for Christ's righteousness. Your perfect parent sent Jesus, not only as fully God, but as the One who fully stepped into human skin and lived in the ocean-deep brokenness of this fallen world. Willing to stoop so low as to walk the earth in finite human form, experiencing temptation, pain, sickness, and sorrow, He died on your behalf and rose again to bring you into new life in Him.

When His righteousness covers your sin before the eyes of God, your guilt no longer determines your identity. With the penalty paid, you can stand before God without shame because you wear the robes of Christ's righteousness.

A Practice of Holiness: Repentance

When you break God's law and sin against Him, you should experience guilt, but if you repent of your sin, you do not have to live in shame. For the first eight years of my parents' marriage, my dad was very angry. Although he was a believer, he had bought into the lie that anger was just part of his personality, and people around him would just have to accept him as he was.

Because my dad saw anger as a personality defect, he was either burdened with the responsibility to fix himself or buried by the shame of a defect he could do nothing about. When the Holy Spirit opened his eyes to how his anger was actually sin, he repented and finally experienced freedom from shame. The subsequent change in my dad's life was nothing short of remarkable. I was born a few years later, and I have never thought of him as angry. Shame forgets who you are in Christ, but guilt welcomes you to repent and become more like Christ.

Walking in the righteousness of Christ feels like fancy, spiritual stuff, but it begins with knowing who Christ is and repenting of who you are without Him. This is the practice of recognizing your status as a new creation. Emmanuel, "God with us," is the ultimate example of who you can be when walking in right relationship with God. Right before the list of virtues in 2 Peter 1, Peter calls believers "partakers of the divine nature," meaning we have been washed clean from sin and given the Holy Spirit to grow us in holiness. If we make a habit of daily repentance, we will experience a deeper dependence and intimacy with God.

1. Study the life of Jesus in the Gospels.

If you are to be more Christlike, you have to know what Jesus is like. Jesus came to be the perfect human you wish you could be. The goal of all our efforts at godly motherhood should be that our hearts are transformed to be more like His. Jesus didn't just project perfect humanity; He lived it from the inside out. You need to have that same kind of heart and to act out of that kind of heart. It is especially helpful as a mom to make note of how Jesus treats others, that you may grow in treating your children with the kind of love Jesus lavished on others. Intimate knowledge of how Jesus loves people creates a heart that is soft toward God, quick to recognize your sinful impulses and repent of them.

2. Be sad over your sin.

After the Holy Spirit opens your eyes to your sin, the first step of repentance is to grieve. Second Corinthians 7:10 says, "For godly grief produces a repentance that leads to salvation." This isn't being sorry that you got caught or sorry that the consequences of your sin are painful. This isn't sadness over losing your status of being a "good mom" in the eyes of the world. When King David repents of his sin in Psalm 51, he says "Against you, you only, have I sinned and done what is evil in your sight" (v. 4). Godly grief leads to repentance because it is sorrow over sinning against God and breaking your relationship with Him.

3. Say your sin.

It's tempting to gloss over your sin because the process of godly grief is painful. When the Holy Spirit opens your eyes to your failure to follow God's path, don't use nice names for your sin, like comparison instead of envy or frustration instead of anger. Correctly identifying your sin and its wrongness is essential if you are to experience both the full weight of your sin and the bounty of God's grace. Again, in Psalm 51 King David says, "For I know my transgressions, and my sin is ever before me" (v. 3). David does not just admit his sin to himself, but also shares it with the greater body of believers through this psalm. Whenever possible, don't just say your sin to yourself or in your journal, but share it with a trusted friend, that you may experience accountability. Identifying your sin takes humility, but humility allows you to lay down your self-made crown and put God back on the throne of your heart.

4. Turn to God.

The purpose of repentance is to turn away from the sinful path of your selfish heart toward the better path of intimacy with God. Once you stand in sorrow over your sin and admit that you have broken God's law, the Holy Spirit empowers you to turn away from your sin toward God. When God is in His proper place on the throne of your heart, you will experience freedom from shame.

Dear Ashamed Mom,

God counts Christ's righteousness onto you. Do not linger in the shame of the world for not measuring up or constantly stand as your own accuser. Jesus' work redeemed you before a Holy Judge. Accept His work and repent of your sins to grow more like your glorious Savior.

P.S.

Read Romans 7 and 8 to see the apostle Paul's inner war with sin and the gift of life by the Spirit.

CHAPTER 6

STRESSFUL STANDARD:

You're a good mom

GOSPEL TRUTH:

Become more like Christ

In 2014, I posted a picture on social media of myself and my three boys, who were then three and under. An acquaintance posted an overused comment, "Supermom!" and I staggered under the weight of it. If she only knew what my life looked like, she would never call me that. I was a physical and emotional mess, failing at everything I deemed important: a clean house, kind words to my children, even Bible study. I was in survival mode to the extreme. Our culture's favorite commendation for women is "You are enough!" or its motherhood counterpart "**You're a good mom!**" But these encouragements come with a heavy burden to bear.

No matter how many times people tell us that we're doing great, we see our failures every day. We struggle with the inauthenticity of it. Deep down we know that our circumstances often get the better of us. We know that the mom who yelled at her children for putting on their socks too slowly (true story—and it's happened more than once) isn't a particularly good mom. We know if you stay up too late scrolling Instagram, you're not going to have enough energy to get the kids to school, do a full day of work, then come home to make dinner and drive your kids all over the world for their activities with a happy heart.

It doesn't take a degree in psychology to identify the root of the problem. It's us. We make bad decisions. We are self-focused. We overextend ourselves. We are sinners. Most days we aren't particularly good moms if we hold ourselves up to our society's standards.

For some reason, people keep on telling us we're good moms anyway, which not only makes us feel like failures but also frauds. We're ashamed of our inconsistencies and hidden imperfections. "You're a good mom!" makes it worse instead of better. We become worried about people seeing too much of our lives and discovering that we don't measure up.

A GOOD MOM'S KINGDOM
IS NEVER GOOD ENOUGH

In a world where every mom is told that she's a good mom, but few *actually feel* like one, we become stuck in shame. We worry that the hobbled-together kingdom we've built just isn't enough. "Good mom" shame builds up in motherhood. What we've messed up in the past starts to dictate our future. This is the same reason I am afraid to go to the dentist.

I couldn't go to the dentist for about eighteen months because I had two pregnancies right in a row, and it felt like there was no point (actually, one particularly bad dentist I saw while pregnant with my second son told me there was no point in going while pregnant—bad dentist! Bad dentist!). Eighteen months of pregnancy followed by three kids three and under and grandmas who were afraid to watch all three babies at the same time led to three years. I know it's ridiculous—I could totally go to the dentist, but the shame of putting it off for so long keeps me from making the call. There's a brick wall built by my self-shaming thoughts: *Why had I let it go so long? And why don't I ever manage to floss my teeth?* It's hard to admit, but it has now been over six years since I've been to the dentist (I'm so sorry, Mom; don't shake your head at me), and I still keep putting off the appointment.

My latest excuse is that I can't give up a writing morning. I only get two mornings each week to write without distraction, and I have manuscript deadlines looming, so how could I possibly go to the dentist (or floss my teeth at night, right?). I mention these things to my husband, and he reasonably offers to come home early from work so I can go, but that just makes my shame double. Has it really come to that? It's not actually that I don't have time to go to the dentist. It's really that the shame of not having gone for so long has built up like plaque, making it hard to move forward. Shame breeds avoidance.

This is my silly proof that you're wrong if you tell me, "You're enough." I'm not even enough to make a dentist appointment. We're not going to talk about my pantry or my car or grace-filled parenting or godliness. We're just talking about the dentist here, people, and if dental shame can be stifling, motherhood shame can bury us.

When we place our identity in being "good moms," shame becomes our constant friend. We must keep up the appearance of being good at every single momming thing or else someone might recognize the crumbliness of our kingdom. When we hear a fellow mom (especially one we admire) make a comment that begins with "we always . . . " or "we never . . . " and we realize that we never do the things her family always does or we always do the things her family would never do, we get a knot at the pit of our stomach and question our worth.[1] When our identity is built around the structure of our family, we strive to also build the facade of mom perfection so that not one little word from an acquaintance can fell it.

When we let our motherhood successes and failures define us, we end up with shame buildup all over our lives. No matter our lists, goals, and action plans, we'll never quite measure up. We make mistakes. We forget to sign that field trip form. We let anger and unforgiveness simmer against our children. We let half-truths fall from our lips instead of taking the time to answer our kids' earnest questions well. We fall back on frozen chicken nuggets when we've planned organic salad for dinner. Then we start seeing messiness in our own children—personality short-comings, sin, or simply developmental growing pains—and we attribute that messiness to our own.

On the outside we plaster on a smile while desperately trying to hide ourselves and our family life from the world's judgmental eyes. How can we be considered a good mom when there's so much that we don't do right? We hide in a cloak of busyness. Just keep doing all the things and no one will ever see what we're really like.

But Jesus died to be our spiritual dentist (stick with me here). He wants to wipe back the shame, but even underneath all that plaque, our teeth are pretty rotten. So, He pulls out each rotten tooth and replaces it with a shiny new one. Now we stand before God with high-wattage celebrity smiles. God won't shame us if we've been avoiding His gentle but sometimes painful care. There's no reason to avoid God because His love isn't based upon our actions. He is always ready to forgive our wandering. God is the King of the second and seventh and millionth chance. He can make all these old, shameful things we bring Him new in Christ.

Even my shame-ridden heart and my plaque-ridden teeth. I think I'll go make that appointment now.

ENOUGH IN CHRIST

Do you know that Jesus lived a fully human life just like yours? While still fully God, He became fully man. He dressed Himself in human skin and experienced all the trials of life on earth within the confines of humanity. And still He did not sin. I dare to guess that if I took a walk in Jesus' sandals, I would have sinned at least 1,278,376 times in His lifetime. But not Jesus. His sin count was zero. Jesus' life is the ultimate example of virtue and goodness.

That's good news for moms! You get to stand before God clothed in Christ's righteousness like a designer gown on Oscar night. Not just good—beautiful. In Christ, your identity isn't broken and failing but forgiven and freed.

Praise the God who makes us shiny and new *in Christ*. Ever noticed how those two little words are sprinkled throughout the New Testament? It's like a New Testament author can't end an idea without them. These two words don't only communicate the imputation of our sins onto Christ, crucified—a glorious fact, for sure, but one we shouldn't stop at. "In Christ" offers us the glories of double imputation—meaning that on the cross, Jesus bore the penalty for our sin, and because of that, we have Christ's righteousness credited to our far-overdrawn bank accounts.

You'll never be enough by your own power. In Christ you are declared righteous, but that doesn't mean there isn't still a lot of work to do. You are a new creation that is still being made new. You are already righteous *in Christ*, but you are also undergoing sanctification and becoming *more* of what you are in Christ.

In the last chapter, I told you that God is always at work in you, even when you keep falling back into the same sin patterns. That is the reality of grace, and it motivates us to move forward in repentance. God does not give up on you, but the paradox is that you still have work to do. You are in Christ, but it is the work of the Christian life to become more like Him.

BE TRANSFORMED

Most people believe that it is completely their responsibility to change themselves, but that is not the process of sanctification— how a believer changes to be more like Christ. Dr. David Powlison, a developer of biblical counseling, explains that there are five factors that work together to create sanctification in the life of a Christian:

- God
- biblical truth
- suffering and struggle
- wise mentors
- yourself[2]

Because all five factors may be present in motherhood, it has the possibility of creating significant transformation in your life. First, if you are in Christ, God is at work within you; that is always a constant for believers. Also, motherhood leads to real suffering and deep soul struggles, and those pressures help you see your sin more clearly. You change through hard experiences, not through comfort and ease, and motherhood is nothing if not hard. Motherhood is not only hard but also complex, so it has probably led you to seek wise counsel from mentors and friends.

The hardness and complexity of motherhood should also lead you to seek out a deeper understanding of God's Word. Finally, motherhood makes it evident that you are not perfect, and in the process of sanctification, recognizing your weakness can motivate you to work toward heart change. You are the final factor in your sanctification, and you can either respond sinfully to the pressures of motherhood or recognize how the Holy Spirit is moving you toward change and choose to battle against your sin.

James calls this being "doers of the word, and not hearers only" (James 1:22). Doers of the word aren't working to repay

God's salvation but responding with worship to what Christ has done for them. "But the one who looks into the perfect law, the law of liberty, and perseveres, being no hearer who forgets but a doer who acts, he will be blessed in his doing" (James 1:25). If you are in Christ, you don't work by your own power; instead, God's commands for morality in both the Old and New Testament become a law of liberty—an avenue for freedom and blessing.

A Practice of Holiness: Virtue

About fifteen years ago, my dad got his first flex fuel SUV, one that could be powered by either traditional gas or ethanol. I was fascinated when I noticed the little sticker on the back of the car.

"Dad! You can get E85 now!" I declared.

He frowned and said, "Why would I? It gets terrible mileage."

He was right. On average, cars get about 10 percent fewer miles per gallon on E85.[3] Have you ever seen someone fill up their car with E85? Me neither.

Truisms like "You're a good mom" or "you are enough" in the face of staggering evidence to contradict them are bad fuel. They might keep you going for a while, but they don't create optimal performance. Grace, on the other hand, is superfuel. As you see the depth of God's grace, you long to be more like Him. You no longer work hard at motherhood to prove your worth or repay God's kindness. Instead, grace motivates a life of worship through the daily work of motherhood. I am fueled to follow Peter's admonishment to add virtue (2 Peter 1:5). This is also translated moral excellence or goodness. Two verses earlier it is applied to God and translated as His excellence: "His divine power has granted to us all things that pertain to life and godliness, through the knowledge of him who called us to his own glory and excellence" (2 Peter 1:3). I can be virtuous, morally excellent, and good because God has granted me all that I need to live with godliness just as I know God's glory and moral excellence.

Instill these practices in your life to grow in virtue:

1. Fill your mind with good things.

It is hard to love virtue and righteousness when you are always filling your mind with the world's wisdom. Paul admonishes the Philippians: "Finally, brothers, whatever is true, whatever is honorable, whatever is just, whatever is pure, whatever is lovely, whatever is commendable, if there is any excellence, if there is anything worthy of praise, think about these things" (Phil. 4:8). Excellence in the list above is the same word translated virtue, moral excellence, and goodness again. You can't expect to be fully immersed in the culture of the world, obsessed with what it proclaims important, praiseworthy, and beautiful, and not have it affect your actions. When you fill your mind with songs, podcasts, and books that proclaim the glories of the gospel, you will be drawn toward righteousness.

But you also don't need to throw the baby out with the bathwater (a disturbing metaphor at best). There are good things that exist in the world that are not overtly Christian but can turn your heart to Christ all the same. In her book *All That's Good: Recovering the Lost Art of Discernment*, author Hannah Anderson writes: "Our life on earth, all the things we experience, all the work we do, all the good things we enjoy, aren't simply a hurdle to the next life. They are designed by God *to lead us* to the next life. They are designed to lead us to Him."[4]

So, pursue the things that are good in this world as an opportunity to know your Creator.

2. Seek God in matters of conscience.

Motherhood is full of decisions that are not explicitly outlined in the Bible, but that doesn't mean that you are not equipped with the wisdom you need to make those choices for your family. "If any of you lacks wisdom, let him ask God, who gives generously to all without reproach, and it will be given him" (James 1:5). As you seek to make good decisions for your family, seek wisdom through knowledge available about the subject via science or other earthly authorities, diligent study of the Bible, and the conviction of the Holy Spirit through prayer. We must make careful decisions while still allowing for God to lead us to different convictions. We may be all across the board in school choice, political views, cultural engagement, and habits of health, but we can still be united in the truth of the gospel.

Dear Not-Enough Mom,

In Christ you are dead to sin and alive to God. You have eternal life. You are free from condemnation. You are free from the bondage of sin and the punishment of death. You are His temple. You have the unconditional love of God.[5] Knowing who you are *in Christ* motivates you to become more *like Christ*. So, you should make every effort toward not just outward displays of godliness, but a heart transformed to be more like Jesus—loving the things He loved, hating the sin He hated, and serving in God's kingdom with wholehearted abandon.

P.S.

Study the words "in Christ" or "with Christ"
and "through Christ" in Ephesians, noting how
each mention informs your identity.

CHAPTER 7

STRESSFUL STANDARD:

Be more than just a mom

GOSPEL TRUTH:

Find your life by losing it

I'm in a mid-motherhood crisis. My middle son is about to start kindergarten, and my youngest is only one year behind him. By the time you read this book, I'll be a daytime empty nester. People say that motherhood is still a full-time job even after they are in school, and I believe them. I never shut off the mom part of my brain—even when I went on a weeklong cruise with only my husband to celebrate our anniversary. I never stop being mom, in my brain and with my being, even when my kids aren't with me.

I also know that I could easily fill up the hours when they are gone at school. There are about a thousand things I could be doing better at home. I certainly could spend many more hours a week keeping the house clean. I could make more of our food from scratch so there would be less preservatives in it. I could actually exercise. I could always shower more often and put on makeup more than once a week. I could cut coupons and shop at multiple grocery stores instead of choosing the most convenient. I could lead Bible study and serve more in my church. Hey, I could even write more books or do more ministry on Instagram or update my blog more than once in a blue moon. It's not that I don't think I can fill up the school hours.

It's that I wonder if it would be enough. Busy enough to not feel guilty about not homeschooling my kids. Useful enough to not feel like a nonessential drain on our family's resources. If I fill up my hours in those ways, will I be content with my life? Will I be important and meaningful? If my boys are gone for the majority of the day, will I still experience the joy in parenting that I do now? Without their needs and their constant attention, will I still feel purposeful? Or should I seek other work? Should I work a few hours for the family business or build my mentoring program for writers or edit a blog for a parachurch organization? Will I be happy if I don't do more? Will it be enough?

The world usually tells me it won't. *Don't be just a mom. That will never satisfy. If you want to be yourself, you need to **be more than a mom**!* The church often says the opposite: *Be a stay-at-home mom. Your greatest mission field is at home!* I know the "right" church-y answers to my questions of identity and value, yet they still linger in my subconscious and produce an underlying anxiety about my future.

The world adds to the pressure of motherhood by telling us that we should pursue our own happiness. We may even become moms because children are *supposed* to bring happiness, joy, and meaning. Where once parenting was considered a role and duty, it has now become an experience from which we expect to receive the benefit of joy. We become stuck in this paradox, because while motherhood can feel meaningful, fulfilling, and fun, all parents know that more often, parenting is plain, old-fashioned hard work.

In her book titled *All Joy and No Fun: The Paradox of Modern Parenting*, journalist Jennifer Senior explains the change that happened in parenting in the twentieth century and has informed our understanding of motherhood in the twenty-first century:

> Until fairly recently, what parents wanted was utterly beside the point. But we now live in an age when the map of our desires has gotten considerably larger, and we've been told it's our right (obligation, in fact) to try to fulfill them. In an end-of-the-millennium essay, the historian J. M. Roberts wrote: "The 20th century has spread as never before the idea that human happiness is realizable on Earth."[1]

Just about the time a mom comes to grips with the idea that motherhood will never fulfill her (usually when the second or third child is born or her oldest hits elementary school), she discovers a second rule just waiting in the wings: if motherhood doesn't fulfill you, find what does.

Society's answer is to follow your heart, discover your passion, and achieve your dream. Happiness becomes a burden that we are responsible to fulfill on our own. We control our own destiny, so we can navigate our ship onto the seas of our best life if we have the gumption to do it. Don't be just an average mom, be *more than a mom.*

This self-help gospel is at the core of our own kingdom building. We must work at achieving our goals no matter the cost: hop on the latest diet or exercise fad, attend webinars on how to build an Instagram following and launch your online business, write the book, start the podcast, travel the world. In the kingdom of mom culture, this is the only life we have, so we must live it to the fullest.

However, our kingdoms built on self-centered dreams are crumbly, disappointing places. They're never quite big enough to make us happy. No matter how much time we hustle, they always feel a bit subpar. Happiness remains elusive. If we could just get more followers, the promotion, the number on the scale, the leadership position at church or my child's school, then we'll be happy. But these things will never quite satisfy. *We will always want more until we experience the God who is enough.*

KINGDOMS FULL OF EXPECTATIONS

When we rely on this stressful standard of motherhood to save us, we often create a kingdom of kids. We tell ourselves, "If I just fully immerse myself in creating their perfect lives, I'll experience true purpose." We get FOTMO (fear of them missing out) when we see other families' awesome vacations, summer bucket lists, intense sports involvement, or expensive music lessons.

But if we fail to create the perfect childhood experience for our kids or don't experience joy in motherhood, we're tempted to give up. We focus on surviving the day instead of living for God. We think *I'm exhausted from the hustle, so I'll just quit trying. I think I'll just lie down amid the toys and clothes strewn all over my floor in my hole-y sweatpants and take a nap because this whole motherhood thing is the end of me.* We long for previous seasons when we controlled our own lives. We want to live without the pressure to be more than mom or to find happiness in a relationship with a child who doesn't have a fully formed brain. This is what comes from holding tightly to our lives: exhaustion, worry, and despair.

Our kids are not strong enough to support the weight of being the center of our universe. When we focus on creating magical childhoods, we may miss the calling of God in other areas of our lives and fail to teach our children what it means to love and serve others in the kingdom of God instead of themselves.

KINGDOM OF SERVICE

There is happiness to be found in this role that requires so much servanthood. In Matthew 16:25, Jesus flips our expectations on their head: "For whoever would save his life will lose it, but whoever loses his life for my sake will find it." If you expect to find your life in motherhood, you won't. What you *will* find there are endless opportunities for service and sanctification.

Focusing on yourself will not lead to satisfaction. In the next verse He asks, "For what will it profit a man if he gains the whole world and forfeits his soul?" (Matt. 16:26). You'll never save your life by trying to be *more* than whatever God has called you to be.

The little happiness that the gifts of the world offer make it hard to see the greater joy before you. Conversely, loosening your grip on finding your purpose and experiencing happiness makes it easier to see the glory of the One who came to give you life to the fullest (John 10:10). After all, your Savior lost His life to make yours new. When you follow the example of Jesus, you will discover that lasting happiness comes from walking in fellowship with God.

Consider the apostle Paul. If there was ever a man who had practically everything going for him, it was pre-conversion Paul. He was the best Jew around. He had every reason to be confident in his own abilities (Phil. 3:4). If he was living today, his Instagram would have perfectly candid shots of ritual sacrifices with his fellow Pharisees, a daily Instagram live featuring his word-for-word recitation of the Torah, and well-lit photos of his trendy sandals on the rustic temple steps.

He was living his best life, until he met Jesus and realized the depth of his own sinfulness and his inability to be righteous by his own power. After the road to Damascus, Paul shed his old identity to accept Jesus' death and resurrection as his own. This death to self sounds a bit horrifying, but Paul flips the script: "Whatever gain I had, I counted as loss for the sake of Christ" (Phil. 3:7). From the perspective of the world, Paul had gained the whole world, but then he met Jesus and realized that it was all loss compared to a relationship with his Savior.

Motherhood offers a painful breaking down of your self-designed, self-focused world. It strips you of the ability to have the perfect life by your own power. The world says you will discover happiness by putting either your children or yourself at the center of your world. God offers His Son to be the firm foundation for your happiness, no matter your circumstances.

A Practice of Holiness: Godliness

In Peter's list of virtues for a godly life, he includes godliness. When I first read this, it felt too obvious. If you want to be holy, pursue godliness, but I discovered that it meant having reverence or respect for God; it's the New Testament equivalent of fearing the Lord. When you have proper reverence for the greatness of God, His grace, and the gospel, you willingly lay down your small, inconsequential kingdoms to serve in the eternal, unparalleled kingdom of God. As you serve and worship your rightful King by daily laying down your life, you will finally experience the happiness you have been searching for. You can build a reverence for God by adopting these simple habits in your life:

1. Change your vocabulary to reflect your source of happiness.

The things of this world are not meant to give you life, but to point you to the Life-giver. It's tempting to throw around the popular phrases like "_____ is giving me life right now," or "_____ is everything," but your words inform your thinking. Nothing in this world can give you life; it was purchased for us with Jesus' death on the cross. Your kids, your husband, your job, your ministry, your favorite books, essential oils, a new song, a cup of coffee, the perfect new rug—none of it is a sustainable source for life. All these things need to remain beneath the throne of your heart, or they will actually begin to take your life away by taking God's place in your life.[2] You experience life when you cast even the wonderful blessings of God at the foot of His throne and proclaim *only a relationship with Jesus gives me life.*

2. Do the work God puts right in front of your nose.

I've not walked in a season of motherhood that wasn't marked by some kind of limitation. Yours may be entering into first-time motherhood, being a homeschooling mom, having a child with behavioral challenges or disabilities, enduring your own physical suffering, or working at a job you don't like or longing for a job you can't have. These grace-filled limitations are often God's tool for clarifying your calling. It may be a season or it may just be a day, but God is equipping you to do what He's called you to do, and the calling of His kingdom often looks different from what the world or your own heart imagine. If you stop longing after the fun or fancy calling of the woman on social media or in the next church pew, you can grow to enjoy the work God has called you to do today, instead of longing after the next season.

My friend Sarah is both a gifted creator and administrator. She can take an idea from concept to fruition in a way that astonishes me. I am among many who are consistently blessed by her willingness to use her gifting in service to others. Still, she cannot do all she'd like in this season. While most of the women around her are sending their children off to school, she still has little ones at home. On top of that, Sarah has a husband who travels often for work, and she is going through some painful physical limitations. She works a part-time job with little help of childcare and has dreams of building her own business. She has the capacity and the talent to do so much, but she's been forced to slow down.

Instead of anger or bitterness at these roadblocks, Sarah is living fruitfully within her current sphere of influence. She works hard at the tasks God has given her and proclaims God as the Lord of her life by leaving the plans for her future in His hands.

When another friend, Beki, sent her children off to school, she looked no further than the needs of her local church. Instead of trying to dream up her own plan, Beki asked how she could help. She already served as a pianist, but Beki's church needed someone to play bass guitar, so she spent hours learning and practicing in order to serve in that capacity.

3. Pray about what you want.

I'm not telling you to throw up your list of must-haves for happiness at God like a genie who will grant your wishes (let's be real, we have all done it at some point). Instead, pray that God transforms your heart's must-have list to be all about Him. Ask God for help building more reverence and respect for His glory and His good plan for your life. It's a simple prayer that I promise He will answer: "God, help me want You more than I do now, and more than this world." This kind of prayer is always within God's will. The process won't be easy, but it will lead to happiness.

Dear Longing-for-More Mom,

The secret to happiness *can be found* in life outside of motherhood. However, it can't be found in the transient joys of this world, but in God Himself. Worry less about finding your happiness in what you can accomplish and start focusing on obeying God's clear callings today. Then you'll experience the happiness of fellowship with God, because you were made for exactly that kind of "more."

P.S.

Consider how 1 John 3 describes the way you should act in light of God's love for His adopted children. These respectful responses are His will for you, today, no matter your season.

CHAPTER 8

STRESSFUL STANDARD:
This is your only chance

GOSPEL TRUTH:
God's grace can redeem
your insufficiency and quiet your fear

On my oldest son's first day of kindergarten, he happily hopped out of the car in the school drop-off line, swinging his big-kid-sized backpack over his slim shoulder. He turned, smiled, and waved. My heart pounded. He was ready; I was a mess. How could this boy be excited to be gone all day? How would I survive not knowing what he was up to? He ran in, and I reluctantly drove away, the doubts creeping in as I turned out of the school parking lot: *Was he fully prepared for school? How would he measure up to the other kids? Was he behind in reading? Would he obey the classroom rules? Would kids be nice to him? Would he be nice to them?*

The deeper questions weighed me down until my shoulders slumped and my chest ached: *Did I do enough? Was he prepared for kindergarten academically, physically, emotionally, and spiritually? Did we make the right schooling choice? Did I mess something up? Will it be too late to fix it? Did I fail so atrociously at the first six years that he will fail at life?*

As our children grow up, it feels like our momming abilities are uniquely displayed to the world through our kids' actions. When your children are little, most people (except that persnickety woman next to you at the restaurant) dismiss the antics and disobedience of our children. Even when your daughter is throwing wood chips in the air on a playground, a fellow mom will console you: "It's okay, she's just little." But as our kids get older, the burden of their actions lies more squarely on our shoulders. We feel judgment in the email from school about our child's discipline issue. We are ashamed when our children act out in public or end up in the remedial reading group. We've been told, **this is your only chance!** So, every hurdle feels like we've blown it.

On our best days as moms—the days with few discipline issues and kids who thank us for making dinner without prompting—we take comfort in this rule. We may believe that because we have worked hard, we are reaping the fruit of godly children. In the future, which feels both so far and so close, we'll look at our adult children and see them committed to the Lord, serving in the local church, invested in their marriages, and raising up the next generation of believers. We long for a Proverbs 31 woman experience, where "her children rise up and call her blessed" (Prov. 31:28). The joy of our grandchildren as they run into the church nursery will be a testament to our faithfulness in motherhood.

In our idealized imaginings, our kids will be the evidence that we didn't fail at this motherhood thing after all—proof that we were discerning, took every opportunity to teach the gospel, and fed them all the right spiritual *and* physical food for them to grow up into healthy and holy adults. Christian kids are basically the A+ on the report card of godly motherhood. Their holiness seems indicative of ours. Our pride tempts us to attribute goodness in our children to our hard work instead of the work of God in their hearts.

At least that's how we feel on the good days. On our worst days, we fear this rule. If this is our only chance, then surely we've ruined our kids. If they do accept God's free gift of salvation, they'll probably struggle with the same sin patterns as us for the rest of their lives. All we've really done is set them up for failure in their walk with the Lord. In this scenario, the weight of their salvation rests on our shoulders.

A KINGDOM OF KARMA

In the kingdom of mom, you are responsible for your salvation *and* your children's. If you are a "good" mom, you'll reap good (even godly) kids as a reward. If you don't live up to the specific brand of motherhood you aspire to, then your kids will be ruined. But the world isn't driven by karma. Everything doesn't have an equal but opposite reaction. If you believe the world is ruled by cause and effect, you will not persevere when circumstances don't make sense. When you know that God's grace redeems brokenness and His sovereignty uses broken situations to make you whole, you will persevere because He is trustworthy and faithful.

God doesn't follow the cause-and-effect script of karma. The grace of God can cause sweet strawberries to grow in bad soil. God isn't held down by the world's rules for how things work. The grace of God can raise up godly kids from sinful parents. He brings life from death. He redeems broken sinners with His holiness. He shines light into dark places. He leads stubborn hearts to repentance at the foot of the cross.

A MISPLACED IDENTITY
AND HOPE FOR US

My cousin Erin is a homeschooling mom with four children. She lives on a large country lot and taps her maple trees to make her own pure maple syrup. I don't even buy pure maple syrup at the grocery store (give me the fake stuff in a jar shaped like a happy grandma any day), but she makes her own while homeschooling four kids. And you should see her garden—it's beautiful!

My childhood best friend Betsy is a guidance counselor at a local middle school. She pours herself out to care for the physical and emotional needs of her students while keeping her three athletic sons in sports, and she still gives up her time to serve in the high school ministry at our church.

I used to be intimidated by these two women. I'm sure you know other moms you admire but whose outward accomplishments intimidate you too. Maybe it's the mom who's physically fit or the mom with the high-stress corporate career or the friend who runs a full-time business while staying at home with her kids.

The truth is that another mom's abilities have nothing to do with your value as a mom. When my identity and hope for motherhood are not in what I do or don't do, but in Christ Himself, I don't have to be intimidated by awesome moms like Betsy and Erin.

The mom that you are idealizing may not have the same struggles as you, but she does struggle. I bet she also has a mom that she admires and wishes she could be more like. No matter how good you are at your brand of motherhood, you will always sit in the darkness of shame when you put your hope and identity in motherhood instead of God.

The world is full of opportunities to ground yourself on something other than God. Motherhood feels like it is everything. I'm not just talking to stay-at-home moms here. You carry motherhood around with you even when you leave your children in the care of others or they grow old enough to watch themselves. How could it not start to become your identity? How could it not become your hope?

We *know* that Jesus is the only firm foundation for our hope and our identity, but we feel the constant pull to find our hope and identity in the performance of our children. What should you do when motherhood keeps turning your head? It's a simple answer, but outrageously challenging to do: keep turning your focus back. Wrestle to keep God at the center of your life instead of your children. I know you're probably thinking: But how do I do that? Don't worry. I'm going to take this broad concept down to the practical in the next chapter.

A MISPLACED HOPE
AND IDENTITY FOR OUR CHILDREN

I really love re-gifting, mostly to my cousin Crissy. Neither of us have sisters, so I call her my sister-cousin. (Don't get that confused with sister-wife; that's an entirely different kind of thing.) Because I know Crissy so well, I sometimes get a gift that I like but know that she would truly love. So, when her birthday or Christmas rolls around, I've already got the perfect present, unused, ready to give her joy. I don't hide the fact that it's a re-gift. She does the same for me. Recently her triplets had a birthday, and my boys gave them a load of our old toys, and her kids couldn't have been happier. We're passing along the joy of re-gifting to the next generation.

Unfortunately, we can't re-gift God's grace. I can't give my identity in Christ to the children I love so much. My faith cannot become theirs. Sometimes, no matter how much work I do directing a child to the holiness and grace of God, I watch them persist in a sin pattern. I can neither control their sin nor create their sanctification. Their sinfulness doesn't mean that I have failed, but that they need grace! Each of my children must face the reality of their own sin and the beauty of God's grace and receive the gift of faith from God so they can receive the gift of salvation.

An unbelieving child may be a Christian mom's biggest fear. As we fight to entrust our children to the care of God, it lingers in the depths of our hearts. *What if, after all that I've done, all my service, all the hours of hard work to teach them the gospel, my children don't know the Lord?*

I recently met a mom named Colleen, a mentor of one of my dearest friends, who watched her daughter accept Christ at a young age, then turn her back and follow the path of the world well into her twenties. Colleen did all the right things when her children were little. She memorized verses with them. She told them the goodness of the gospel. She pursued the Word of God in her own personal study. Despite her best efforts, her daughter still wandered from the truth she had known. Ultimately, there was nothing Colleen could do to ensure that her daughter was saved. Colleen told me that all her tears, prayers, and struggling over her daughter's actions came down to one final question: *Is Jesus still better?* Through much emotional pain and sanctification, her heart finally believed that He is.

A few years after Colleen came to a deep abiding trust in God, He finally moved in the heart of her daughter. Not through any work of Colleen's, but through a parachurch organization wholly unconnected with Colleen or her church. Instead of living in fear of possible future outcomes, like Colleen we can ask ourselves: *Even if my worst fears are realized, is Jesus still better?*

A Practice of Holiness: Perseverance

Our identity as citizens of heaven is not secured by the good works of well-behaved children but by the work of Christ Himself (Phil. 3:20). He is our hope, our identity, and our great inheritance. Because He is a steady foundation, Peter encourages us to remain steadfast (2 Peter 1:6)—also translated perseverance (NIV), patience (NIV), and endurance (NLT). These steps will help you persevere in the face of great challenges:

1. Expect to wait.

The fifteen-month-old child of a dear friend just spent a few weeks in the hospital. When I would visit, her mom would tell me that the hardest part was not knowing exactly what was wrong with her daughter or how long they would be there. All she could do was trust in the God who knows. Sometimes that trust faltered, but it also got her through. You probably aren't comfortable with lingering in the unknown—a quick Google search usually clears up concerns or questions. You probably enjoy the instant feedback of social media and the ease of Amazon Prime free shipping. Our lightning-fast world rarely requires you to wait for anything. On the other hand, the Bible is full of waiting. No matter your translation, the word "wait" appears over one hundred times. In an essay on waiting titled, "Maybe This Year?" Elisabeth Elliot says,

> Instead of seeing His everlasting love, tenderly bending down to our humanness, longing over each of us with a father's speechless longing; we sometimes think of Him as indifferent, inaccessible, or just plain unfair.
>
> The worst pains we experience are not those of the suffering itself but of our stubborn resistance to it, our resolute insistence on our independence.[1]

If you want to grow in the practice of patience, you need look no further than motherhood. You may have to wait for your kids to eat their dinners, on the doctor to correctly diagnose a persistent illness, for your next career advancement, or for the slow cashier at the grocery store. Taking a moment to mentally step back and submit to God's sovereign lordship over your circumstances in prayer can transform an expectation for immediacy into patient endurance.

2. Focus on God's faithfulness.

When you find yourself looking ahead with anxiety to a possible future where your children don't know Jesus, force yourself to look back to this morning and yesterday and last week, and ask yourself: *Is He faithful to equip me and accompany me for every challenge I face? Is He better than anything else I desire?*

He is. He has proven Himself faithful from the beginning of time until today. As God proves Himself daily, in the littlest ways, your faith becomes steadfast. If the day comes when one of your children rejects God, you'll have a foundation of who you know God to be built up under your feet. It may be the most painful thing you ever experience as a mother, but it doesn't have to cause you to lose faith in God.

Dear Gospel-Sharing Mom,

Righteous children are not your inheritance despite all the hours you spend teaching the gospel, discussing and explaining theology, or redirecting wayward hearts. Indeed, in Jesus you have *a better inheritance*—unbroken relationship with God Himself, available to you in part on earth and in completion in heaven. As theologian John Piper says, "The gospel is not a way to get people to heaven;

it is a way to get people to God."[2] Even if you face the pain of wandering children now or in the future, in Christ you will always have the perfect love and acceptance of God.

P.S.

Pray Psalm 16 to remind your heart
of the glories of God's presence.

CHAPTER 9

STRESSFUL STANDARD:

You don't have time for quiet time

GOSPEL TRUTH:

Intimacy with God is essential

In 2010, controversial performance artist Marina Abramović sat at a simple table and stared into the eyes of strangers for her exhibit "The Artist Is Present" in the Museum of Modern Art in New York City. People waited hours for the opportunity to sit across from her in silence. Abramović did not speak or move other than slightly bowing her head when each participant chose to leave the table. She just remained present in that space with that stranger by looking them in the eye. People waited in line for hours to participate.[1] The popularity of the exhibit demonstrates the natural human longing for the attention and presence of others.

We all want to be drawn near to others. I experience this nearly every morning as a mom. I hardly ever wake up early enough to finish my Bible study before my kids get up. It is a rare day when my time studying God's Word goes uninterrupted. One by one my boys come and snuggle up against me as I sit on the large wingback chair in my home office or the cushy couch in our living room. I tell them to grab a book to look at as they wait for me to finish. I expect them to sit in one of the empty chairs across from me, but they always plop themselves down on my lap or wedge themselves in next to me. They want to begin their day in my presence, to feel the gentle rhythm of my beating heart, to experience the security of being smushed up against my warm legs and enveloped by my arms. I love when they grab one of their Bibles and we sit together—I trying to decipher complicated passages or praying or finding comfort in God's words, they looking through pictures and remembering the stories they represent—all of us entering the presence of God together.

When our mornings don't begin like this, a different atmosphere permeates our home. Each of us is quicker to attend to our own needs, to snap in response to a request, or withhold grace in the face of an offense. We were made for connection, presence, and intimacy. If we do not have it, we long for it and experience the side effects (or sin effects) of its lack.

Theologian J. I. Packer explains that God is not just omnipresent (everywhere at all times), but that He is a God who is "present with his people—namely, God acting in particular situations to bless faithful folk and thus make them know his love and help and draw forth their worship."[2] God was *with* His people in the Old Testament, and Jesus came as Emmanuel, "God with us." Believers get to experience *God* with us through the working of the Holy Spirit today. We need His presence.

Back in the garden, Adam and Eve experienced true intimacy with God. Walking with Him in the cool of the day, learning from Him without the barrier of sin. But because of the fall, our world and our hearts are broken. We ignore the presence of God and experience an emptiness in our souls. We try to fill that hole with people and things and experiences that will always be second rate and ineffective at filling the void. We need God's presence to be holy and to be happy, and the Holy Spirit is always working to bring us into it. As the eyes of our hearts are enlightened (Eph. 1:18), we begin to recognize the glory of our inheritance in Christ.

Packer writes that through a knowledge of God's presence, we will experience "personal fellowship with Jesus," "personal transformation of character into Jesus's likeness," and "the Spirit-given certainty of being loved, redeemed, and adopted through Christ."[3] Nearness to God creates more fellowship with Him, sanctification, and an assurance of who we are in Christ.

The good work we do in God's kingdom leads to opportunities for us to depend on God, which leads to our sanctification. David Powlison defines sanctification as having "your faith simplified, clarified, and deepened."[4] When we feel the depth of our inability to do the work before us on our own, faith is simplified. We must trust the One who empowers us, or we cannot move forward. When we read the Bible and learn about who God is and how He acts, our faith is clarified. When we see God's careful involvement in the circumstances of our own lives, our faith is deepened.

People think they are letting you off the hook when they encourage you that it's okay, *you don't have time for quiet time* in this busy season of motherhood, but what we hear is that it is impossible (or at least improbable), so we shouldn't even try. This diminishes mothers. If a mom can manage to keep all of her people fed for the day, get them off to school and activities, keep the household running smoothly, and pour herself out in whatever job or ministry she does, then she can also apply her creativity to identify unused spaces to meet with God. No, it may not be forty-five minutes alone doing inductive Bible study before her children wake up (or it might be!), but meeting with God is not relegated to a comfy chair beside a fire with a cup of coffee. Quiet time does not have to be quiet. It can be listening to your Bible app and praying on the drive to work. It can be memorizing your Bible verse as you shower. It can be a worship music dance party as you make dinner. *Do not* give up experiencing the presence of God in any season, no matter the circumstances.

KINGDOM OF MISPLACED MOTIVES

I've said it one million—okay, one hundred—okay, maybe ten different ways in this book, but I'll say it again: the fruitful motherhood you're after doesn't happen when your focus is on building your own kingdom. Unfortunately, the shift in our motives is subtle. Even as I write this book, I sense the instability of my own heart. There have been days I sat down at my little red laptop and tried to build my own kingdom through these pages. I put all my effort into being a fancy writer with all the writing chops to build a perfectly turned phrase that could speak to your hearts. Every time I place my fingers on these keys, I am faced with my own selfish motivations. I want you to think much of me. I want this book to define my purpose as my kids launch into the world of full-time school. I want to be a good enough mom to justify writing books about motherhood.

On the days when my heart is not first satisfied by God, I'm instead motivated by my own kingdom and my own glory. The work that I'm doing looks the same, but the fruit is decidedly different because my motives are wrong. Writing is slow and tedious. I try to present myself as one who has it all together instead of vulnerably sharing the places I'm still learning. I'm quick to shift the focus of my words from God's truth to my big ideas.

So it is with motherhood. We can do the same kind of good work on two different days, but our motives can differ drastically. We may exert our power with intense self-focus, or we more covertly honor ourselves under the guise of building God's kingdom. Instead, we're really working from our own resources for our own glory instead of *through grace for God's glory*. Because we are powered by self-reliance and control, the first thing to fall off our ever-lengthening list of to-dos is entering into the presence of God. We tell ourselves and each other that we're just too busy to meet with God in this season. It's just one task too many.

When we work hard, we expect results, but fruit only comes from relationship with God. If we want to have a meaningful and lasting impact on the world, we must turn our attention from the good work we can accomplish to experiencing intimate relationship with God *through* the good work of God's kingdom.

From this intimacy we experience the fruit of the Spirit in our lives. Can you imagine the kind of impact we could have as moms if we were exhibiting fruit like love, joy, peace, patience, kindness, goodness, faithfulness, gentleness, and self-control

(Gal. 5:22–23)? Instead of motherhood bringing the attention and honor to us, it would point others to God. When we let go of having to be exceptional in our own right, we can experience the exceptional love of God, the immeasurable grace bought by Christ's work on the cross, and the intimate fellowship with God made possible by the Holy Spirit's work in our minds and hearts.

SIGNS OF MOTIVATION

Our motives are at war within us, and they will never be perfectly pure. As the words of "Come, Thou Fount of Every Blessing" say, we are prone to wander. We are prone to leave the God we love.[5] How I wish it weren't so. I wish I could just stop my wandering once and for all. I long for heaven, where my heart will stay stubbornly focused on its joy in Christ. But until that new world, I must learn to recognize when I'm wandering, so that I can turn back more quickly to God. I've noticed five signs that my heart has turned to building my own kingdom.

First, *I fail to meet with God.* I sleep past my morning time to study the Bible. I don't read the pretty verse cards leaning against the window behind my sink. I forget to pray in the car as I drive my children to school. Although I may not realize it at the time, I'm subconsciously avoiding God or anything that reminds me of Him, because I just don't want to submit to His lordship. I've fooled myself into thinking that my way is easier or better than God's.

Second, *my thoughts turn inward.* I rant about how others have hurt me or neglected me. I tell myself all the things I deserve for all the hard work I'm doing. I make lengthy, lawyer-like arguments justifying my actions toward others and my pursuit of my own comfort. My thoughts have one focus: me.

Third, *I am unable to love others well.* A few weeks ago, I got all huffy with my husband. His best friend's wife was out of town, so they wanted to take all the kids to the gym pool together. I was hurt. My reasoning? My husband had been out of town the week before and each of us had an obligation every night that week, and I missed him. I thought that because my husband wanted to come alongside his friend, it meant that he didn't care about me. When I focus on my needs and neglect meeting with God, I feel poured out and dry, so I respond to the simple needs of my children or husband with anger and impatience.

Fourth, *I want the world.* I can't quench my desire for new clothes or household décor. I long for the quick comfort of my phone or some chocolate or a bubble bath. When my desire isn't fulfilled by an intimate relationship with God, there is no end to my wanting. I am no longer content with the earthly blessings I already have. I take stock of the blessings of others—usually via social media—in an attempt to discover what will make me feel whole.

Fifth, *I obsess over fixing my sin myself.* Instead of expressing godly sorrow over sin and following the steps of repentance, I do my best to fix it without involving God in the process. I vacillate between shame and pride as I boldly try to do battle against my failures by my own strength. But self-help never works. The first step in killing sin is identifying my sin, which requires some self-focus, but the following three steps—"fixing our hearts on God, meditating on God's Word, and praying often"[6] all transfer my attention from myself to the glory and power of God. Whenever I spend more time dwelling on my actions—good or bad!—than on God's character and kind love for me shown in the gospel, I know that my heart is wandering.

These five glaring signs of a wandering heart have something in common: unhappiness. There is no joy to be found in personal comfort or motherhood or the gifts of this world or being a better person apart from Christ. Even as Jesus gives the Sermon on the Mount (Matt. 5–7) on how to live under the new covenant, He is concerned about the heart behind our actions. As He admonishes us not to be anxious about our own needs, Jesus gently reminds us, "Seek first the kingdom of God and his righteousness, and all these things will be added to you" (Matt. 6:33). When we seek our own kingdoms, we will always be unhappy, but when we set our minds on God's kingdom, all of our needs will be met, and our desire satisfied in Christ.

MOTIVATED BY THE PRESENCE OF GOD

The presence of God is the right motivation for your good works. What is particularly problematic about living for the kingdom of mom is that it gets the purpose of motherhood all wrong. God made you a mom not because He knew you would be awesome at it, but because motherhood is one of the ways God uses to teach you your need of Him and grow you in knowledge of Him. This purpose for motherhood transforms your motives from serving and glorifying yourself to knowing God through the good work He has given you to do.

You may wish you weren't so broken. You might wish you could get your act together. You may long for freedom from sin or just the ability to get the physical work of motherhood done more efficiently. Maybe you create plans, goals, and rules to force your imperfect soul into submission, trying to conquer everything that you think you are failing at because God's work of sanctification in your heart feels like it is taking too long.

When you are frustrated by the plod of your sanctification, you probably have the wrong reason for growing in holiness and doing fruitful work. What originated as the holy motivation to be more Christlike likely has warped into a desire to be successful, to look good to others, or to gain the approval of your spouse or children. In short—you guessed it—you have begun to build your own kingdom again.

Godly motherhood is the fruit of God's work within you. Instead of starting with who you want to be and what you want to do, begin with who Christ is and the work He has already done. Paul tells the Philippians to "work out your own salvation with fear and trembling" (2:12). Why should they work hard? "For it is God who works in you, both to will and to work for his good pleasure" (2:13). So work hard but make certain your motivation is the work God is already doing in your heart. Paul asserts this again after he describes what it means to fellowship with Jesus: "Not that I have already obtained this or am already perfect, but I press on to make it my own, because Christ Jesus has made me his own" (3:12–13). Like Paul, you can press on in your sanctification and good works because of the work Jesus has already completed to make you one of His followers.

FELLOWSHIP WITH GOD

Only God knows the number of hairs on my head and the number of times I have told my kids to stay near me in a parking lot. It's one of my least favorite parts of motherhood. My boys are too old for me to insist that they hold my hand, yet too young for me to trust them to navigate a busy parking lot without my safe presence. When we exit the car into the dangerous minefield of our church parking lot on Sunday morning, I insist that they remain near me. *Don't get too far ahead! We need to look both ways. People can't see you! Don't dawdle!* Surrounded by distracted drivers, I know that the safest thing for my boys to do is remain with me.

In John 15, Jesus commands us to "abide" in Him. Most of us are familiar with that word, but also confused by it. When's the last time we've heard the word abide outside of Christian contexts? My guess is it was the zero day of the month of never in the year of nonexistence. So, thank you, Holman Christian Standard Bible translation for using the word "remain" instead. By remaining in Christ, we experience fruit (John 15:4–5 HCSB). Abundant fruit! *Fruit of change* in our own hearts and *fruit in others* from displaying the glory of God to them and *fruit of serving* the kingdom of God faithfully—more fruit than a farmer's market in July! All this good fruit is produced when we remain in God.

Regrettably, we tend to make remaining in Christ more complicated than it really is. If it's hard to enter God's presence, then we are still bringing something to the table. Fortunately, God refuses to let us remain in our self-righteous efforts. He made coming into His presence simple through prayer. We can do it out loud or in our heads, bowed down beside our beds or driving in the car, using Scripture to guide our words or groaning out the depths of our emotion before God. Don't even know what you need? No problem! Jesus Christ and the Holy Spirit are currently at work interceding on your behalf (Heb. 7:25; Rom. 8:27, 34).

Remaining isn't that complicated. That's why I'm mystified by how many times I must exhort my boys to stick with me in one trip through the church parking lot. We need a lot of reminders to remain too. The world is distracting. Just concentrating on one thing in the midst of everyday motherhood can feel impossible, but if life is complicated and circumstances are hard it's like we're standing on a rock in the middle of the ocean during a hurricane. *Of course* it will take some effort to keep our feet firmly planted in hard seasons! Conversely, a lack of challenging circumstances can make remaining difficult too. It's hard to train our attention on God when life around us looks shiny and exciting. Whether it's challenge or boredom that plagues us, remaining isn't passive.

WORKING HARD IN GOD'S KINGDOM

Remember, *if we remain in Christ, then we bear much fruit* (John 15:5 HCSB). I have some fruit (well, vegetables, if we are going to be precise) growing in my backyard right now. For years, I've wanted to have a vegetable garden, but I've been too afraid of my lack of gardening skills and knowledge and the possibility of failing. In the back of my brain I've been hoping that my mom (who, you remember, lives next door) would just do it for me. The raised beds my husband built are technically on her property anyway. This year I finally realized that I would never have the homegrown produce I longed for unless I stepped out in faith and did the work.

As my boys tossed seeds with the haphazard carelessness of a child on a mission into the small divots I had measured and plotted, I knew deep in my soul that there would be no fruit without the hand of God upon our work. After we finished, we prayed for God to bring the rain and the sun and His grace upon the land to create fruit from our insufficient efforts. And He did. Not every plant grew, but we still received an abundant harvest by His provision.

If we want to receive the fruit of the Spirit, we must plant and weed and fertilize and water. Then God, in His mysterious and miraculous ways, sends the sun.

One of the unexpected gifts of this process of God-powered fruit-bearing is that it releases us from the tyranny of shame. Like many moms, I am in a love-hate relationship with my smartphone. My phone helps me fit my ministry into moments of the day that might have passed unused. I wrote the rough draft for my first book on my smartphone while sitting in the playroom with my young children, directing their play, acting as toy referee, and occasionally engaging in their games. I don't think my kids need to have all my attention, every moment of the day.

Unfortunately, my phone often leads me to distraction more than it does productivity. I fall down the wormhole of social media or Google news. My kids pull on my arm, begging for my attention, but I barely register their existence because of the Buzzfeed article I'm consuming to learn if I'm a true child of the 90s. I shudder to think what this communicates to my children about their value. I hate to realize what it says about the true desires of my heart when I grab my phone for a quick social media scroll mid-Bible reading.

I haven't done away with my smartphone altogether, but I'm learning that building boundaries for my phone usage produces fruit in the relationships. Still I am far from perfect. The siren song of social media calls to me as I eat lunch with my son, and I often give in. I get a little twitchy at the idea of watching an entire show with my husband without looking at a second screen. I haven't yet left my phone charging in my bathroom instead of at my bedside as I've intended.

Some days I flourish within my limits, others I ignore them completely, but God's redemption means I don't need to fall into a shame spiral every time I make a mistake. I can repent from sin that results from unbridled phone usage and continue working hard at following God. The fruit of these boundaries may not be exactly what I expect, but when I follow the leading of the Holy Spirit, it will come. Ultimately, it is grace that makes any good works or good fruit happen. I need grace to start and grace to finish, and grace for my sins in the middle and grace to enable my good works and produce fruit in me too.

The apostle Paul understood that it all begins, continues, and ends with grace, so he begins his epistles with a prayer for grace and peace to come to his readers and ends each letter with "Grace be with you." The Holy Spirit inspired Paul to sandwich all his exhortations toward righteousness with grace. (Paul must have understood that a sandwich is garbage without great bread.) Your good works begin and end with grace. Without grace, you'd be left with something ineffective and insufficient. All the good things we do flow from what Jesus has already done for us. Make a practice of sandwiching your good works with God's grace by incorporating prayer as you work. Prayer is an opportunity to submit your plans and efforts to the lordship of Christ and experience the fruit of His kingdom.

A Practice of Holiness: Effort

When Peter exhorts you to "make every effort to supplement your faith with virtue, and virtue with knowledge, and knowledge with self-control, and self-control with steadfastness, and steadfastness with godliness, and godliness with brotherly affection, and brotherly affection with love" (2 Peter 1:5–7), he asserts that the purpose of these qualities is to "keep you from being ineffective or unfruitful in the knowledge of our Lord Jesus Christ . . . for if you practice these qualities you will never fall. For in this way there will be richly provided for you an entrance into the eternal kingdom of our Lord and Savior Jesus Christ" (1:8, 10b–11).

Moms don't want to be ineffective or unfruitful, but there is an even more essential reason to practice the qualities on this list of virtues: they help you enter into the eternal kingdom of God. This isn't about salvation; it's about daily taking part in God's kingdom through a relationship with Him. Faith, virtue, knowledge, self-control, steadfastness, godliness, brotherly affection, and love are descriptors of what it looks like to be holy. These two practices build a relationship with God that will bear fruit:

1. Practice "remaining" rhythms.

The most practical way to fix our attention on God is to make regular appointments with Him throughout our day. These remaining rhythms remind us to look up from our belly buttons and into the glory of the Lord. They attach a spiritual discipline to an already established daily routine, such as praying for your family while you're brushing your teeth. Listening to a Bible app on the way home from work. Memorizing a verse when you're at the kitchen sink. Take some time to consider how you could create opportunities to connect with God throughout the day. Go slowly; habits are created over time. Adapt as needed for different seasons of the year or of life. Give grace. If you have ten rhythms for meeting God during the day and you get to five of them, that's great! Five times you met with God when you may have forgotten Him altogether.

2. Utilize Bible study techniques that fit your season.

I recently wrote an article titled "5 Bible Study Techniques for Busy Moms" that outlined a few different methods for doing Bible study no matter your circumstances:

- Read one psalm when you wake up, get back to the Word if you can
- Study one chapter at a time in depth for a long time
- Read lots of chapters quickly, looking for one or two common themes
- Memorize and meditate
- Study with a group[7]

Don't neglect the study of God's Word during busy seasons, but do not be afraid to use a different method than you have in previous seasons.

Dear Purposeful Mom,

If you don't make time and space to be drawn into God's holy presence, you will work yourself to the bone and still have nothing to show for it. It is the work of the Spirit of God to create fruit in the rocky soil of your heart and the hearts of your children. May you work to establish rhythms of remaining that will produce eternal profit.

P.S.

Circle every occurrence of the words "abide" or "remain" in John 15. Write down the results of abiding and not abiding in Christ.

CHAPTER 10

STRESSFUL STANDARD:

*You're not supposed to be
your kid's friend*

GOSPEL TRUTH:

*Your children are
your nearest neighbors*

Last winter, I was angry. Not just an occasional annoyance but bursting with anger every day as I loaded my three sons into the car to leave for school. I hated being angry, but I couldn't manage to break free from it. I asked my friends for strategies to get my kids into the car more quickly, I took deep breaths, I allowed for more time to get the plethora of coats, hats, mittens, bags, and snacks on our persons and out to the car. No matter what I tried, I couldn't stop my explosions of anger. I became desperate. I didn't want my children to grow up with a mom who yelled at them. I was afraid that other people would find out, friends or followers would soon know that the woman who was talking to them about being a godly mom was anything but. I felt stuck, like nothing I could do would break the cycle.

All my well-intentioned tactics failed, because I was more focused on how unfair my circumstances were than my own sin. I placed a lot of blame for my anger on one of my sons in particular. This boy does everything else fast. He runs everywhere, is the first kid done with dinner, and speeds through his schoolwork. He is like a gazelle, sprinting through life, but as soon as I announce, "Boys, it's time to go!" he becomes a sloth. He dons his shoes and coat so slowly that I could create a stop-motion video of him. It takes a lot of effort to leave the house as slowly as he does. When I'm not so angry, I can find the humor in the irony. But not last winter. I was in a catch-22. If I stopped to discipline him, it would only make us later. I tried talking to him at another time of day and would be convinced I had gotten through to him—until the next morning. Watching as he slooowly turned the sleeves of his coat right-side-out was enough to send me over the edge. I'd get in his face and demand, "Just get it *together!*" as he refused to get any of his things together.

I took these slow-motion power struggles personally. I told myself: *He doesn't respect you. After all the ways you serve him all day, he can't just do this one thing to honor you. He'd obey if it were his dad telling him to get out the door. You deserve better treatment after all you do for him. Why can't he just get in line and give you an easy morning for once?*

My anger felt justified because his disobedience was personal and perpetual. Even when I apologized for my anger, his actions never changed. I kept a mental record of his past wrongs, and I let my anger build up until I was constantly on the edge. Because I had not forgiven him for his past mistakes, I was unable to forgive him for his present disobedience.

AN UNFRIENDED KINGDOM

The world assures us that we're not supposed to be their friend, wisdom that was originally meant to help us set and enforce good boundaries for our children, but that often warps into a justification for unkind actions. This has birthed memes like "I'm not your friend. I am your parent. I will stalk you, lecture you, drive you crazy. I will be your worst nightmare and hunt you down when you need to come home, because I love you." Although it says these actions are done in love, the attitude of this popular meme pits parent and child against each other and condones boundaries without empathy. It's easy to fall into the trap of a combative, rather than loving relationship because it often feels like our kids are out to get us when they are just learning to live within the good boundaries God places around our lives.

Moms experience a lot of *personal* disobedience. You know the kind I'm talking about—when your child pretends they can't hear your admonishment, or worse yet, they stare at you as you give an instruction, then proceed to ignore it completely. What you think will be a simple teaching moment escalates. They may call you names or hurl painful insults. They may withhold their love. This same child may readily obey their dad or grandparents or be the favored teacher's pet. You wonder why it's just you and start to feel your own bitterness grow in response to theirs. When a child's disobedience seems personal, responding in love can be challenging.

Moms experience a lot of *perpetual* disobedience. It's usually not the second chance that we have a hard time bestowing; it's the 39th chance or the 578th chance that feels like too much. The repetition makes it hard to extend grace. Such disobedience wears away at our ability for unconditional love. The child who doesn't want to stop playing to do her homework is easier to forgive than the son whose homework creates a daily battle. As we walk in close relationship with our children, their bad habits and sin patterns rub up against us constantly.

In the face of perpetual and personal disobedience, you may want to withhold forgiveness. Although unforgiveness only extends your suffering; there are four reasons you may intentionally or unintentionally withhold forgiveness.

1. *Control:* You're the mom, so you're supposed to be in charge. When your behavior solutions or discipline strategies do not produce change, it feels helpless. You may harbor unforgiveness toward your child because your response is the only thing you can control.

2. *Blame-shifting:* Withholding forgiveness from your children puts the onus on them. It says that if they would just behave properly toward you, you could behave properly toward them. It relieves some of the pain of your own sinful actions within the conflict by focusing on the disobedience of your child.

3. *Punishing Others:* You've endured the cost of their sin, but they don't seem to care. Maybe the "sorry" never came or didn't seem sincere. You adopt an icy attitude or withhold small acts of service or take joy in their sorrows, telling yourself *it serves her right* or *now he knows what it feels like.*

4. *Protecting Yourself:* Sometimes a child might say "sorry" willingly and often, but never actually change their actions. Forgiveness feels pointless and vulnerable. Your child has hurt you so often with their unkind words or disobedience that you build a wall because you just can't stand to be hurt again.

All these responses succeed in accomplishing one thing: maintaining your kingdom. When everyone else serves in your kingdom, they bear the brunt of the blame for any pain and discomfort you experience. When you are sovereign, you are the executor of all justice, and you remind others by punishing them when they make mistakes. Your children bear the burden of keeping you happy. Refusing to see your child as a friend keeps you on the throne.

KINGDOM OF NEIGHBORLY LOVE

Instead of coming alongside my son as we tried to get out the door, I lorded my power over him through angry outbursts. God's kingdom offers a better path. You cannot force yourself to love your children enough to never experience bitterness and unforgiveness toward them. You will be quick to harbor these sins against your children when you do not see them as your nearest neighbors. When asked *what is the greatest commandment?* Jesus responded that it is to love our God with all our heart, soul, and mind (Mark 12:30). When we are walking in this commandment, the second flows from it: love your neighbor as yourself (Mark 12:31).

It is always easier to love your own comfort and happiness than to love your children as Christ loves you. In John 15, the chapter on abiding—ahem, *remaining*—in Christ, Jesus says, "This is my commandment, that you love one another *as I have loved you*. Greater love has no one than this, that someone lays down his life for his friends. You are my friends if you do what I command you" (vv. 12–14). When you remain in Christ, you have the ability to love others with the kind of sacrificial love of Christ. This laying-down-life love is defined in 1 Corinthians 13 as a love that is not irritable, and does not keep a record of wrongs (v. 5). The only way a mom whose kids disobey her one hundred times a day can possibly live up to such love is by remaining in Christ, consistently experiencing the great love she has received so she has a great love to give her children.

In a relationship with two sinners, no one is ever faultless. I brought my own sin into those tumultuous, early mornings before school, but continued to blame my children. If they would just be better kids, I could be a better mom. Their sin (disobedience) felt worse than my sin (anger) because it was the initiating action, but before a holy God, all sin deserves death. But praise our perfect God—He offers us the opportunity to come back into relationship with Him (and each other) through repenting and receiving His forgiveness.

Just as we love because God first loved us (1 John 4:19), we can forgive our children's personal and perpetual disobedience when we experience God's forgiveness. Our repentance isn't about the other person's actions but healing the chasm that our own actions put between us and our holy God. Biblical repentance is a microcosm of the gospel.

A Practice of Holiness: Unconditional Love

When my kids dawdled before leaving the house, my feelings were hurt. I refused to look beyond my own pain to discover that in fellowship with God, I am never unseen, my hurts are not overlooked, and I have access to an always forgiving kind of love to share with my nearest neighbors.

The list of virtues in 2 Peter encourages you to work at love. Your kids require more than the easy kind of love—the sweet giggles over an inappropriately timed toot or the gentle snuggles of a sick child. They need the continually forgiving, bitterness-fighting, laying-down-your-life love of God expressed to them through your actions. When you live in relationship with a wholly loving and forgiving God, you receive an abundance of deeper than deep love. You can practice this kind of special love for your children until it becomes a habit of your life:

1. Make allowances for immaturity.

The older your children get, the more tempting it is to hold them up to adult expectations or assume they have adult motives. If your child is lashing out against you in a way that feels very personal, pray for grace for their immaturity. They often do not know the depth of hurt they can cause or are responding out of desperation to hurt you because even good discipline often feels painful.

2. Process the problem with God.

If you immediately go to your friends for help, you miss out on the opportunity to hear from God. You may become fixated on creating a behavior in your kids instead of seeing how God wants them to grow. When you bring your problems to God and ask for His guidance, you receive wisdom that goes deeper than the latest discipline strategy (James 1:5).

3. Say you're sorry.

Perfect parenting moments are few and far between. I rarely go through an extended discipline circumstance without sinning against my child. When you say "sorry" and ask for forgiveness first—even if your child is "more" in the wrong—you demonstrate the gospel to your kids. After a confrontation with your child, take the time to pray, asking God to humble your heart so you can see your own wrongdoing instead of focusing on your child's disobedience. When your heart is truly humbled before God, you will be able to say "sorry" first, even if you did not do the first or the worst offense.

Dear Unforgiving Mom,

Your sorrows are not overlooked. God sees every way you have been wronged, and He offers you comfort and acceptance when you feel rejection and dismissal. Jesus Christ experienced unbelief, ridicule, and rejection, then chose to sacrifice Himself for all who violate His law, reject Him, disobey Him, and dishonor Him. He bore God's wrath for your disobedience. Because of His forgiveness, you can worship Him by offering forgiveness to the perpetual or personal disobedience of your children.

P.S.

Consider what 1 John 3–4 says about God's love
for us and our love for others.

CHAPTER 11

STRESSFUL STANDARD:

*Mom and Dad have to be
on the same page*

GOSPEL TRUTH:

*You can be united in your motivations
despite your differences*

As I prepared to write this chapter, I asked women on social media to finish the sentence, "My husband and I aren't on the same page about _____." The responses were all over the place. Some were funny; others were incredibly serious. Many involved parenting and discipline, but some involved long-term planning, housework, money, and relationships. Although the answers were as diverse as the backgrounds and marriages of the women submitting them, I realized that every woman reading this book will likely have a running mental list of rules and convictions where they are not on the same page as their husbands.

Even my husband, Wes, sent in an answer: "Number of back rubs." As you might have guessed, he is not talking about the number of back rubs *he* should give *me* per week. I informed him that we would never be on the same page on the issue of back rubs since he is hoping for more than one a day, but that I was willing to live with that discord. We had a good laugh about it, but we've had plenty of topics where we were not on the same page in our marriage that were no laughing matter.

From the beginning of our marriage, we disagreed about how many children we would have. He thought we should have two or possibly, maybe, if he had to, three—max; I definitely wanted three but really longed for four. For years I didn't worry about it too much, because I expected he would ultimately cave to my desire for four. Eventually, what had once been a low-level background hum of disagreement throughout the childless years of our marriage became a cacophony of discord after we had our three sons in a little less than three years.

Like I've mentioned, I *really, really, pretty please with sugar on top* wanted a daughter. Unfortunately, after three boys born in such quick succession, I didn't have any energy to even consider having another child for a long time. Once my youngest was almost three, I started to wonder if God would bless us with one more child (maybe the dearly longed-for daughter would finally arrive), but Wes couldn't make up his mind. What followed was a year of emotional hemming and hawing. I would give up hope, then Wes would make a comment that seemed like he was coming around and my heart would do a happy dance; then he would take it back again, and I would be devastated. I prayed and prayed and prayed for God to miraculously intervene or change Wes's heart.

Growing your family can never be a one-sided decision, so I was caught between the strength of my desire for another baby and a husband who just wasn't on the same page. We both had solid points on our side of the argument, and this wasn't a case of a clear mandate from God on how to proceed. In the face of a stalemate, Wes suggested we take the month of December off from talking about the issue to pray, then come back together and discuss. I quickly agreed, certain that God could change Wes's heart if only Wes would seek Him.

As I came before God and prayed about our family's future, I was humbled by His sovereignty and sufficiency. He chose to give us three boys born closely together. He ordained that I would not receive a daughter but would instead know His Son better through that experience. As I celebrated Christmas with a fresh humility, God gave me a peace with the makeup of our family in a way I had never experienced. I could hardly believe that God hadn't changed Wes's heart, but mine.

Shortly after Christmas, Wes and I discussed the future of our family and finally found ourselves on the same page. Wes confessed that at the beginning of December, he had also thought we would likely try to have one more child, but that God had solidified his confidence in the completeness of our family throughout this season of dedicated prayer. Through humble hearts and by God's grace, we were finally on the same page.

I hesitate to tell you this because our example wraps itself up in a bow pretty nicely, and there will be plenty of circumstances when you and your husband will never end up on the same page. The story I shared with you was only a few short paragraphs on the page, but in actuality took ten years of marriage and partnership to work out. I can assure you, that bow was a long time coming.

THE DISUNITY OF OPPOSING KINGDOMS

I was meeting with a group of young moms, discussing what it looks like to parent alongside our husbands who are different from us when one mom quietly asked the question everyone was thinking: "Do my husband and I always have to agree?" Common wisdom says that **parents need to be on the same page** or their children will be confused about standards or sense that the parents are seeking to undermine each other. In this scenario, in order to have a united marriage, you and your husband must agree on everything. This is an impossible standard, because no one in the world agrees with someone else on every possible decision.

So, you may try to force unity by insisting your husband bow to your plans. If he doesn't understand your superior wisdom, then it's your job to fix him: strong-arm him into reading that parenting book, send him to counseling, or withhold sex until he gets on board. If your husband doesn't meet your expectations for parenting or godliness, it's your job to bring him up to snuff. The weight of your husband's choices rests on your shoulders. The health of your marriage becomes your sole responsibility. As you struggle under the pressure of getting on the same page, disunity and discord grow. If he would just do things your way, then your whole life would be better.

You may battle for control over the direction of your children—Whose discipline method will you implement? You may compete over who works the hardest—Who is willing to do the most work around the house after the kids are in bed? You may fight for your own comfort—*Why can't you just watch the kids for a few hours on Saturday so I can have time alone at a coffee shop?* You may even vie for the affection of your children—Will your children love you best or trust you more if you give in to their desire for a new toy or a piece of candy when your husband would say no? If you try to force your husband to agree with you in every detail, you will live in opposition, but if you are both focused on building God's kingdom, you are on the same team.

UNITED IN GOD'S KINGDOM

By now you've seen a pattern: God's kingdom just doesn't jive with the self-focused thinking of our culture. Although we commonly see our husbands as different from us, God created us for unity. In Genesis 2, God declares Adam's first response when he sees Eve is "bone of my bones and flesh of my flesh." (After naming all the animals as different from him, Adam sees Eve and names her "Woman, because she was taken out of Man" [v. 23]). He looks at Eve and says, *she is like me*. Adam and Eve are alike as image-bearers of God. "God said, *'And let them rule. Man and woman are designed to rule together.'"*[1] When any two people are seeking to follow God's plan, they will make different choices and act in different ways, but they can still be united in the same goal.

Husbands and wives who are believers are more alike than they are different because they are both image-bearers and co-laborers in God's kingdom. Focusing on differences creates disunity because we tend to disregard what isn't like us. When we primarily see our husbands as fellow image-bearers, we can relate to their struggles instead of discounting them.[2]

When we find ourselves on a different page from our husbands, we can still empathize with them because we have experienced compassion and love from a Savior who *entered into* our experiences. When Jesus tells us to remain in Him in order to bear fruit, He applies this concept to loving others: "As the Father has loved me, so have I loved you. Abide in my love. . . . This is my commandment, that you love one another as I have loved you. Greater love has no one than this, that someone lay down his life for his friends" (John 15:9, 12–13).

What could be better for a family than a mom and dad who both follow the example of their Savior? Imagine how their family would benefit as they lay down their own needs to meet the needs of the family, speak truth with grace as they discipline their children, offer forgiveness for failures, and work toward restoration of relationship and nearness to each other and their kids and Christ.

When we experience unity despite differences, we affirm that we were made for oneness. "Because we are made in God's image, we are hardwired to love oneness and fear and despise isolation."[3] Although God made Eve because it was not good for man to be alone, marriage is not able to completely fulfill a human's desire for connection. It is a picture of the gospel, but it cannot replace the true good news.

As we look at the Trinity, we see the gospel in its fullness and the goodness of the perfect fellowship with God. The Father loves the Son, and the Son demonstrates that love through coming to earth and literally laying down His life out of love for us. When the Son returned to the Father, He didn't leave us to fend for ourselves. He left a Helper—the Holy Spirit—among us, offering us the grace we need to imitate this self-sacrificial love.

SPECIAL IN GOD'S KINGDOM

It's not surprising that in a world where serving yourself is essential, the role of helper gets a bad rap. If you're setting yourself up as ruler, of course you don't intend to be a helper—that's a role for servants. But when you are working for God's kingdom, you can embrace the goodness of being made not as a god, but in the image of God (Gen. 1:27).

God created Eve because Adam needed companionship. She was his necessary helper (Gen. 2:20), and that role is not separate from her role as image-bearer. "In the Old Testament, the person most often referred to as 'helper' is the Lord."[4] As a mom and a wife, I've spent a lot of time overwhelmed by the sheer volume of help my family needs from me.

When I try to help everyone by my own power, I often fall short. Lately, I've been comforted and humbled by a God *who helps me*. I cherish the words of Psalm 121:1–2, "I lift my eyes to the hills. From where does my help come? My help comes from the LORD, who made heaven and earth." Because I am God's child, He helps me. As I receive the help of God, I can pour out God's love through helping my family.

Unfortunately, you can be helpful while still being motivated by pride. This might look like buying your husband a parenting book that addresses how you'd like him to change, then expecting him to be pleased to receive your "thoughtful" Father's Day gift. Sometimes you complete a home task that he hates (at my house, it's taking out the garbage), expecting effusive praise, and get huffy when he doesn't even notice. As he struggles through a moment of particularly difficult discipline, you might swoop in and "fix" everything with your creative idea instead of allowing time for his approach to work. I've found that often when my husband resists my help, I am offering him the right kind of help with the wrong motives.

The first step toward a humble approach to helping is to pursue intimacy with God. *Remaining* in an all-knowing, all-sufficient, almighty God will humble you. Although your helpful actions may be the same despite your motives, they are transformed through the posture of your heart. When you seek to serve in God's kingdom, you become an ambassador of God's love to your family. By God's grace, He often uses the humble assistance of a wife to soften a husband's heart. Consider how the following helpful actions are transformed by a humble heart:

 Help your husband by identifying his needs like your heavenly Father identifies and meets yours.

If you are maintaining your position of power, you will spend less time considering how to love others. The God who cares for the needs of lilies and sparrows cares so much more for your needs (Matt. 6:25–33). You display the very image of God by providing for your husband's physical needs. It may look like making a healthy dinner or cleaning the room of the house that he uses the most or making it a priority to assist him with the projects on his list for the weekend.

Help your husband by serving him like Christ serves you.

If you are motivated by self-preservation, you will focus on what your husband should be doing *for you*. You may use his in-sufficiency to justify your selfish actions. Counselor Ed Welch explains: "Need other people less, love other people more. Out of obedience to Christ, and as a response to his love toward you, pursue others in love."[5] We are the bride of Christ, and even though He was God, He was willing to serve His bride in His life and death and resurrection (Phil. 2:6–8). If you delight in how Jesus humbly came to earth to lay down His life for you, you find joy in bearing His image in service to others.

Help your husband by pointing him to Jesus like the Holy Spirit does.

When you seek to bear God's image with humility, your goal will be to help your husband *see more of Christ* instead of dictating his sanctification. Create opportunities for your husband to be in God's presence. This may be by sending him off into nature or to a men's gathering at church or making space for him to spend an extended time reading God's Word on a Saturday morning. Leave the work of conviction to the Holy Spirit, but share God's truth with your husband as you learn it for yourself, recount God's work in your own life, remind him of God's faithfulness, and pray for him. This is hard work but bearing God's image always bears fruit.

A Practice of Holiness: Brotherly Affection

In the list of virtues in 2 Peter, you are called to add brotherly affection. It is ironic that the people you are closest to often experience the worst of you. It's so easy to take the affection of your husband for granted. If he is supposed to be loving you like Christ loves the church (Eph. 5:25), then he must have never-ending patience for you despite your actions, right? In Galatians 5:13, Paul warns against this kind of response to the freedom we find in Christ: "For you were called to freedom, brothers. Only do not use your freedom as an opportunity for the flesh, but through love serve one another." Freedom doesn't mean take advantage; freedom means serve others. The gospel creates the ability to treat your husband as both your own flesh and your brother in Christ. These practical habits will help you promote unity between two very different people:

1. Allow your husband to love you.

Looking at this through the lens of *The 5 Love Languages* by Gary Chapman, you may want your husband to love you through service (picking up the kids from school, making dinner, or sending you away for some alone time). You may prefer that your husband loves you with gifts (flowers for no reason or the latest motherhood gadget). You may like him to praise your efforts at discipline or the meal you made. But if your husband doesn't do any of these things, it doesn't mean he doesn't love you.[6] Just as it is good to count the faithfulness of the Lord, it is good to count the small ways your husband demonstrates his love. These healthy love tallies will help you be slower to take offense and quicker to forgive.

2. Seek wisdom from a mentor in your local church.

When you come up against topics or circumstances when you and your husband cannot get on the same page, seek wisdom for your specific experience in your local church. These issues are complex and unique to your relationship, so the wisdom you need will come from another woman who understands your specific circumstance and can speak God's truth distinctively into your life. If you do not already have a mentor in your church, reach out to your women's director or family pastor or ask a woman whose marriage you really admire. Within the local family of God, you will find the wisdom you need to be united with your husband even when you disagree.

3. Pray for One-ness.

You and your husband are one body, and God has given you a physical expression of your union. Yep, I'm talking about S-E-X. I remember when my kids were little, it was challenging to find time and energy for sex. Guess what? Now that my kids are older, it is *still* difficult to find time and energy for sex. Later bedtimes for my kids and earlier mornings for my husband and me mean we must be intentional. Unfortunately, physical unity is one major area where husbands and wives may disagree. I'm not going to make assumptions about whether you have sex "enough," whether you might be the one who avoids sex, or if it's the other way around. All I want to say is that sex is a gift for building unity in marriage, so pray for God to provide space for it and bless it.

Dear Divided Mom,

As fellow image-bearers, you and your husband share the purpose of bringing God glory in all you do. Unity with your husband grows when your focus shifts from yourself onto the heavenly Father who knows your needs and delights to meet them, the Savior who understands the depth of human experience and sympathizes with your weakness, and the Holy Spirit who seals you for redemption and reminds you of the goodness and glory of God. By the power of the gospel, you and your husband can be on the same team even if you are not on the same page.

P.S.

Consider what Philippians 2 can teach you
about relating to your husband with humility.

CHAPTER 12

STRESSFUL STANDARD:

Image is everything

GOSPEL TRUTH:

You are transformed from the inside out

Amy is one of the fanciest women I know. We met in college, traveled through England together, and have an annual tradition of catching up over tea. She's classic fancy: pearl necklaces, nude pumps, red lipstick, and knee-length dresses that duchess Kate Middleton would envy. That was early-twenties Amy. My fancy friend became a mom, and a few years later, a stay-at-home mom. Slowly but surely, some of the fancy was mummed right out of her. Today, jeans and a cute top are "fancy."

Her three daughters have inherited their mom's flare for the fancy. (One is still a baby, but I'd dare to bet she'll follow suit. Or should I say dress?) As a mom of three boys, I find myself living vicariously through her cutesy Instagram shots: flower crowns, fluffy dresses, tea parties, and plenty of pink. Recently Amy shared a story about her oldest daughter begging her mom to dress up fancy for an un-fancy event. She wanted Amy in her fanciest dress, high heels, and plenty of jewelry, as if she were attending a royal christening instead of a ballet recital. But Amy didn't want to stand out in a sea of tunics and leggings. What would the other parents think of her?

As the hour for the event approached, Amy kept experiencing the Holy Spirit's gentle prodding, and eventually decided to lay down the opinions of the other adults in order to please her daughter, and in turn, I believe, she pleased God. Wearing that fancy outfit didn't just say that the opinion of her daughter mattered; it was a step of humility. She considered the work that God had given her as a mother more important than the passing opinions of people she barely knows. I have no doubt that it was a battle fought in the quiet of her own mind against the pressure to find acceptance in this world.

We all fight the same battle to varying degrees. God gave us intrinsic value when He created us in His image, but ever since the garden we have been struggling with our inability to live up to His perfect standard of righteousness. We know that we don't measure up, so we question whether we have any value at all. Like Adam and Eve, we are terrified of standing before others naked and ashamed (Gen. 3:7). We fear being found out, so we erect an image of our best mom self for others to see, attempting to cover our shame with what the world deems beautiful.

When we aren't living in God's approval of us in Christ, we must search for the approval of others to confirm our value. Sometimes it's our husbands or kids. Sometimes it's our friends. Sometimes it's acquaintances on the internet. No matter who it is, whenever we need someone's approval, we give them power over our lives. In *When People Are Big and God Is Small*, Ed Welch admonishes, "What or who you need will control you."[1] The kingdom of other people's opinions becomes the mother country of our impoverished land, so we serve the standards of other people in an effort to establish our own significance.

As we work to portray our best selves to the world, we pass along this standard to our children. They have to wear certain clothes, smile the right way, and pause mid-play as we find the perfect angle for the shot. Even in our most innocuous social media posts we are setting an example that appearances and the approval of others matter. Does that mean we never post pictures of our children online? Some may choose to go that route, but all of us should at least pause to consider what our interaction with social media might be teaching our children.

THE KINGDOM OF SOCIAL MEDIA

Social media is consuming and addicting. We now hold in our hands the ability to both control our image and gauge how others view us. We tend to blame our generation's obsession with personal image on Instagram and its perfectly curated squares, but the problems inherent in social media are a *symptom* of an underlying preoccupation with the opinions of others.

Yes, the perfectly tuned addictive elements of social media add plenty of fuel to the fire, but the spark has always been there. Even now, as I write these words, my phone is nestled in the chair next to me. I am hard at work writing, but I'm tempted to take a quick social media hit—just check if anyone has given me a tidbit of approval in a Like or Follow in the two hours since I last scrolled.

When our value is in our self-made kingdoms, we are constantly comparing ourselves to others and social media is the perfect tool. "We want to hide, but we also want to spy. Spying might reveal the vulnerability of others so that we can believe that they are no different from us (or even not as good as us). Disgrace wants company."[2] Social media plays to this curiosity, this innate desire to measure ourselves against others.

When someone else's life appears so much better than ours, we become discouraged and self-demeaning. We wonder, *Why can't I be that kind of mom?* Or *Why can't I have her life?* Or we put up our own perfect pictures as proof: *My life is just as great as hers.* Or we find our comfort in the glorification of our failures on social media. There's a whole bad-moms movement aimed at helping other moms feel like they're okay no matter what they do because there are other moms out there just like them. We may scroll these accounts to feel like we're not alone, or just because it comforts us to think, *Well, at least I don't do that.*

Social media is a modern-day measuring stick of our worth. As part of the *New York Times* series of articles looking back at the past decade, one journalist considered the perception of motherhood on the internet from 2010–2020. Her findings shed some light on why we feel so much pressure. In the early 2010s, mommy blogging was all about showing the nitty-gritty truth of motherhood, but the advent of Instagram and its reliance on aesthetically pleasing imagery changed the landscape.

"Realness" was mommy blogging's founding currency, and even as bloggers began striving for more polished content by hiring staff and staging photo shoots, they continued to claim that their guiding mission was to provide honest representation — "real" motherhood.... A new set of online mannerisms hardened into place during this era: the duality of maintaining a flawless image while claiming to be nonjudgmental. "Nobody's perfect," this image of motherhood reassures us, adding sotto voce, "except maybe me."

This saintly moment might be the most demanding iteration of motherhood since the Victorian era.[3]

In the era of momfluencers, moms are not only expected to be real and authentic and nonjudgmental, but to look beautiful doing it.

Every time you pop on social media for a "quick second" (read: actually fifteen minutes), you are tempted to hold yourself to the standards of curated social media motherhood. When you compare yourself against everyone on the internet, you'll find that you are always lacking. You can't measure up to the conflicting values of billions of people or even the five hundred people you choose to follow.

THE UNATTAINABLE KINGDOM OF OTHERS

Social media has made mom judgments inescapable:

> Even if you don't go to any parenting-specific sites or
> explicitly follow them on social media, you will be bom-
> barded with other people's firmly held beliefs about how to
> raise children. Someone from high school is so into baby-
> wearing she thinks parents who don't do it are harming
> their children irrevocably (and posts very long Instagram
> captions detailing these views); a celebrity you once enjoyed
> for her messy relationship drama is now extolling the virtues
> of organic children's foods and plying you with recipes;
> someone you don't know and don't remember following
> started his 2-year-old on the violin and is constantly posting
> videos of his lil' genius.[4]

It seems like no matter where you go on the internet someone is either explicitly giving you a rule for good motherhood
or implying one through their perfect photos. As moms realize
the discord that social media sows, many consider a social media
fast or deleting their apps altogether. There are certainly times,
places, and circumstances for such measures, but making rules
won't save you from the deeper issue that is buried in your heart.
If taking a break or cutting out social media allows you to focus
on deepening your relationship with God, by all means, delete
that app. On the other hand, if it's just shoveling dirt over weeds
instead of pulling them out by the root, I encourage you to let
the discontent you are experiencing on social media drive you to

find your value and identity in intimacy with God.

As Paul Tripp says, "we have an awe problem."[5] We tend to worship the wrong things, to care more about the opinions of image-bearers than the God who created them. People-pleasing can yield some short-term fruit, but if the approval of others is your primary motivator, you'll find yourself perpetually insufficient. As the saying goes, "you can't please all of the people all of the time." Even if the people that you want to please are really good, even really *godly* people, fixing yourself for them will never lead to lasting change.

BEHOLDING A FAITHFUL GOD

If you want to be more than a perfect image on a screen, you must experience real transformation. When you recognize the high standards of your holy God and realize how much you need to change, you may try to transform yourself. Self-powered transformation is inadequate to change our sinful hearts.

In his book *Imperfect Disciple: Grace for People Who Can't Get Their Act Together*, Jared Wilson communicates the importance of this concept by "shouting" them at his reader:

> Making your entire Christian life about trying to look
> like a good Christian is a great way to become a terrible
> Christian. Or at least a weak and defeated one. This is so
> important to understand. It is crucially important. It is so
> important that I want to violate a cardinal rule of sophisti-
> cated composition and employ every means of emphasis

that I can to restate it: YOU CANNOT GET POWER TO OBEY THE LAW FROM THE LAW ITSELF!!! POWER TO CHANGE CAN ONLY COME FROM THE GLORY OF CHRIST!!![6]

What good news for rule-following moms! You don't have to make your life about being perfect. You don't have to produce perfect kids. Trying to follow all the rules of the world or even Christianity won't make you a better mom or even a better Christian. Sanctification happens when the motives and desires of your heart are centered on the awesomeness of God instead of proving your worth.

Fighting your behavior isn't enough. You need a total heart transplant. "The average Christian defines sin by talking about behavior . . . Beneath the battle for behavior is another, more fundamental battle—the battle for the thoughts and motives of the heart."[7] When you aim to grow closer to God instead of living up to the good mom standards of the world, you will finally experience both the freedom and the transformation you desire.

"Where the Spirit of the Lord is, there is freedom. And we all, with unveiled face, beholding the glory of the Lord, are being transformed into the same image from one degree of glory to another" (2 Cor. 3:17b–18a). If you want to be a godly mom, there is only one way: beholding the glory of the Lord. Christ has removed the veil that once stood between God and His people. He came to bring God to you in a personal, intimate relationship, and by that relationship you are changed.

UNCOMFORTABLE KINGDOM
TRANSFORMATION

Comfortable lives don't lead to growth. As you remain in Christ, we will experience pruning. "Every branch that does bear fruit [God] prunes, that it may bear more fruit. . . . I am the vine; you are the branches. Whoever abides in me and I in him, he it is that bears much fruit, for apart from me you can do nothing" (John 15:2b, 5). The monumental hardships of life pull back the veneer of your projected image and reveal your motives, but God's most consistent tool of pruning is the mundane circumstances of your ordinary life.

My oldest son recently brought home a piece of art from school that he made entirely from trash. I was shocked by how much I liked it. It was a bit unconventional, but the silver spray paint really did transform those forgotten and discarded objects into something uniquely beautiful. But this unconventional art project motivated my son to hoard trash. He kept every wrapper from his Halloween candy. He gathered little piles of garbage on our kitchen counter and along the baseboard of our living room. Being an okay-ish cleaner, I occasionally threw these piles where they belonged—the trash can—only to receive a barrage of protests from my son days later. Why would I throw away his piles? I told him to stop saving trash if he wasn't going to use it to make something. A few months later we undertook a thorough cleaning of his bedroom, only to find little collections of trash squirreled away in drawers, tucked under stacks of books, and hidden in old gift bags. To me, these wrappers were garbage, but to him they were treasures waiting to be transformed. I gently looked him in the eye and told him that unless you transform it, trash is just trash.

Every mom—working, work-from-home, stay-at-home—spends more time than she ever imagined doing essential tasks that feel unimportant. Like my son's trash collections, these ordinary moments have the possibility of being transformed, but if you coast through them, never considering the attitude of your heart, they are wasted.

If you start to notice yourself grumbling every time you do a repetitive task like washing the dishes or folding the laundry, you might consider what is keeping your heart from being cheerful in the work God has given to you. If you ignore your husband's parenting advice while breaking up a fight among your kids, you might consider how pride is keeping you from receiving wisdom from others. If you tell yourself you *need* or *deserve* a cup of coffee alone in your office or a Saturday afternoon binge-watching the latest Netflix show, you might be alerted to your tendency to consider yourself before considering the needs of others.

If you start to see that God can use your daily circumstances to tear down strongholds in our kingdom of mom, you will see these everyday moments as training ground for big-moment faithfulness. Whether your day is filled with the monumental or mundane, it is meant to prune away your self-centered kingdom motives until what remains is a pure heart that finds its joy in serving and knowing God. Just as your kids will notice when you are using social media to create a perfect image, they will also learn from your example as you grow in godliness through relationship with God Himself.

As Christ works in you, you will grow in the faith and obedience that is pleasing to God. Not by sitting back and just "letting go and letting God," but by working hard by God's equipping grace. If this seems like circular reasoning to you, it is. The Bible never ends with human effort; it always circles back to grace.

Hebrews 11 outlines many great examples of people of faith from the Bible and reminds us that faith is necessary to please God (v. 6), but the author of Hebrews ends the book with this prayer:

> Now may the God of peace who brought again from the dead our Lord Jesus, the great shepherd of the sheep, by the blood of the eternal covenant, equip you with everything good that you may do his will, working in us that which is *pleasing in his sight, through Jesus Christ, to whom be glory forever and ever. Amen."* (Heb. 13:20)

After all that talk on faith, the author of Hebrews reminds us that it all begins and ends with Jesus. Yes, without faith it is impossible to please God, but without God it is impossible to have faith. If all your efforts in motherhood begin with grace and circle back to it, you'll find yourself in the right place.

A Practice of Holiness: Diligence

Because the cycle of grace and effort and failure and grace and effort and grace again can feel exhausting, Peter exhorts you to practice diligence. In this fast-paced world, diligence—"steady, earnest, and energetic effort"[8]—is often overlooked. Although it's never going to be trendy, diligence is necessary if you are to grow in holiness. Sanctification is more slow, consistent plodding toward faithfulness than great triumphant leaps. It requires your steady, earnest, and even energetic effort, and this kind of effort in the face of the mundane requires practice.

1. Celebrate small steps of sanctification.

When you recognize the depth of your need for transformation, you may despair over how much work needs to be done. To protect you from giving up, you should make a practice of recognizing and recording small ways that the fruit of the Spirit are evidenced in your life. By keeping track of your growth, you will begin to see the obvious patterns of the Holy Spirit at work to make you more like Christ. It also serves as a reminder that while you must work hard at growing in holiness, "it is God who works in you, both to will and to work for his good pleasure" (Phil. 2:13).

2. Pray.

Like the influencers and celebrities you follow on social media, you can know a lot about God without really knowing Him at all. No relationship grows through one-way communication. Consider your favorite influencer. Let's say you comment on every picture on her feed and respond to every story with a direct message. No matter how much you may talk to her, you are not friends. But say she responds to all your comments and DMs, maybe eventually you begin to call and text frequently. She gives you advice on your latest discipline problem and you fly out to meet her. You've moved your online friendship into "In Real Life" territory. Your acquaintance relationship has moved into true relational intimacy.

If you only ever learn about God—even if we take gospel truth and try to apply it—you are not living in relationship with God. Prayer adds intimacy to information. Prayer is essential, but easy to skip in an age when your mind is filled to the brim with the content (primarily from your phone). Without it you will not experience real relationship with God. If you don't diligently pursue prayer in your life, you hold God at arm's length. He is the stranger on the internet instead of your perfect Parent, your gracious Redeemer, and your holy Helper.

3. Pursue heart motive transformation.

You have already been made right before God, but you are far from perfect. The right motive for pursuing righteousness is to grow in nearness to God. But don't wait for perfect motives to do the good works God has set before you. Because of the fall, your motives will never be pure. Be vigilant to recommit your heart to following Christ instead of your desires. Pray constantly for a heart that longs to know Him more and serve in His kingdom instead of your own.

Dear Approval-Seeking Mom,

Those pretty Instagram squares and entertaining stories are just a flash in the pan. The images you post there are not indicative of a changed life, and the approval you find there will never satisfy your longing for community and acceptance. When you are transformed into the image of God by the Holy Spirit's work, you will grow in fellowship with the God of the universe. His acceptance is the beginning of the true transformation you are longing for.

P.S.

Read Jeremiah 31:31–34 and Hebrews 10:16–23 and consider how the new covenant transforms your motherhood experience.

My boys love a trip to Grandma's house, even though it's just a short walk up our gravel driveway. Grandmas' houses are magical places, filled with toys that kids haven't grown tired of and treats that moms will not usually let them have. My mom's house is no exception.

I love a trip to my parents' house too. Although I always intend to drop off my boys and head back home to finally get something checked off my list, I have a hard time leaving. I'm drawn in, partially by the comfort my childhood home brings me, but also by the people within. I like to be with my parents, to sit again at their long, white kitchen counter and talk about the inconsequential and the eternal and everything in between. I always walk away feeling encouraged and known.

I hope my boys feel the same way about our house someday. My parents have three children who grew up to love God, so I've asked my mom, "What do you think you did right?" Strangely, she feels like she did almost everything wrong. That if she could go back, with the wisdom she has now, and do it all over again, she'd do almost everything differently. She insists that the way my brothers and I turned out is only by the grace of God.

But I look back at my childhood and see so much that they did right. They were very thoughtful and affectionate parents, neither too lenient nor too strict. They allowed my brothers and me to have a voice in the family, treating our ideas as important and our relationships as valuable. They were willing to admit that they were wrong, and I saw their sanctification firsthand. They were examples of godliness, displaying a passion for God, His Word, and serving in His kingdom.

But I also get it. In her wisdom, my mother looks back at her forty years of motherhood and all she can see is the grace of God. His work shines brighter than hers. It was His love that drew my brothers and me to trust in Him, not her hugs and encouraging words. It was His work on the cross that saved us, not her hours spent keeping our house clean and our stomachs full. It is our fellowship with the Holy Spirit that has ultimately led my brothers and me to grow in godliness, not the hours we've all spent telling our mother about our concerns and receiving her guidance.

Still, her work was and is important. (As, of course, is my dad's!) As she loved us, served us, disciplined us, and counseled us, we learned how God works. Every time she laid down her plans and dreams to serve in God's kingdom, we had a glimpse of God's better plan. The more we saw her shortcomings covered by God's grace, the more we witnessed the glories of the gospel.

In light of this paradox, may we not give up on the hard work of motherhood. So, I pray for you the words of the apostle Peter that you may . . .

> . . . make every effort to supplement your faith with virtue, and virtue with knowledge, and knowledge with self-control, and self-control with steadfastness, and steadfastness with godliness, and godliness with brotherly affection,

and brotherly affection with love. For if these qualities are yours and are increasing, they keep you from being ineffective or unfruitful in the knowledge of our Lord Jesus Christ. (2 Peter 1:5–8)

As you grow in holiness, may you grow in intimacy with God. He is your perfect parent, your graceful Redeemer, and the helpful Holy Spirit. Through intimacy with Him, you will become an effective and fruitful mom, not by following the stressful standards of a broken world, but by serving in the kingdom of God through your role as a mom.

Lots of love,

ACKNOWLEDGMENTS

God first, always. Writing a book and publishing a book are two impossible things that God generously provides the means for me to do. I am wholly dependent upon Him to accomplish this work, and grateful that He equips me to serve in His kingdom through writing.

Wes, you are an even better husband than I realized when I married you. You consistently support my ministry in so many unseen ways. I couldn't do this without you.

Isaac, Zander, and Judah, hanging out with you is the best! It's my favorite, and you're so gracious to send me out to talk to other moms about Jesus. I love growing with you as you grow up!

Mom and Dad, Drew and Dana, and Crissy, you have the uncanny knack of swooping in to love on my kids at the precise moment that I desperately need your help. I'm forever grateful. Mom, thank you for reading early drafts and talking through places I was uncertain.

Abbey, Caroline, and Lauren, you are so faithful to hold up my arms when I am weary. Thank you for your endless emotional and spiritual support. You are a visible image of God's kindness in my life. I'm better because I have you in my corner.

Lauren, your careful edits give me confidence. This book is better because of you.

Sarah, God has uniquely gifted you to support me and my ministry. Your presence, wisdom, input, encouragements, and literal gifts help me persevere.

Amy VZ, the way you ask good questions, listen and respond, and pray without prompting are an endless gift to me. And Ben, thank you for hearing my requests for prayer through Amy and texting me when the stress was heavy.

Those whose stories I've shared, you are so gracious to give me a piece of yourself to put on display as an example to others.

All who prayed, I'm humbled that you would take your own time to bring my work before the throne of God. Thank you.

My team at Moody, I am so grateful to be shepherded by you. It is a joy to work with a group of people who are concerned about being faithful to God's Word and serving the women who will read this book. Amanda, I'm so glad you were willing to sit at my table in the literal and metaphorical sense. Amy, you listen well and are committed to making sure my point of view is heard. I've felt safe with you throughout this process.

NOTES

CHAPTER 1

1. Some of this material was adapted from an article I wrote titled "The Kingdom of Mom." Used with permission. Maggie Combs, "The Kingdom of Mom," Risen Motherhood, December 17, 2018, https://www.risenmotherhood.com/blog/the-kingdom-of-mom.

2. Claire Lerner, "Just Say No to Judgment: How Judging Parents Actually Leads to Worse, Not Better, Outcomes for Kids," Zero to Three, https://www.zerotothree.org/resources/1716-just-say-no-to-judgment-how-judging-parents-actually-leads-to-worse-not-better-outcomes-for-kids.

3. For a deeper discussion on God's purpose for motherhood, see chapter 9 in my first book, *Unsupermommy: Release Expectations, Embrace Imperfection, and Connect to God's Superpower* (Racine, WI: Broadstreet Publishing Group, 2017).

4. Jackie Hill Perry, "The Only Reason You're Still a Christian Is Because Christ Is a Keeper," Instagram, March 4, 2020, https://www.instagram.com/tv/B9U75h1nAR_/?igshid=s5ldah6g4tqy.

5. Hannah Anderson, *Humble Roots: How Humility Grounds and Nourishes Your Soul* (Chicago: Moody, 2016), 199.

6. Perry, "The Only Reason You're Still a Christian Is Because Christ Is a Keeper."

CHAPTER 2

1. Paul Tripp, *Parenting: The 14 Gospel Principles That Can Radically Change Your Family* (Wheaton, IL: Crossway, 2016), 16.

CHAPTER 3

1. Paul Tripp, *New Morning Mercies: A Daily Gospel Devotional* (Wheaton, IL: Crossway, 2014), 10.
2. See also Romans 8:14–15.
3. Elisabeth Elliot, *Joyful Surrender: 7 Disciplines for the Believer's Life* (Grand Rapids, MI: Revell, 2019), 75–76.
4. Drew Dyck, *Your Future Self Will Thank You: Secrets to Self-Control from the Bible and Brain Science* (Chicago: Moody, 2019), 17.
5. Ibid., 39.

CHAPTER 4

1. For more on my story of God's kindness in my disappointment, listen to episode 35 of the *Journeywomen* podcast titled "On What to Do with Unmet Expectations," https://journeywomenpodcast.com/episode/2018/1/6/ep-35-on-unmet-expectations.
2. Paul Tripp, "How Are You Suffering?," PaulTripp.com, November 14, 2016, https://www.paultripp.com/articles/posts/how-are-you-suffering.
3. Oswald Chambers, "The Discipline of the Lord," *My Utmost for His Highest*, posted August 14, 2019, https://utmost.org/the-discipline-of-the-lord/.

CHAPTER 5

1. Edward T. Welch, *Shame Interrupted: How God Lifts the Pain of Worthlessness and Rejection* (Greensboro, NC: New Growth Press, 2012), 2.
2. If you're experiencing shame for what has been done to you, I urge you to seek counseling for your specific circumstances. You can find a certified biblical counselor at https://biblicalcounseling.com/counselors.
3. John Piper, *God Is the Gospel: Meditations on God's Love as the Gift of Himself* (Wheaton, IL: Crossway, 2011), 34.

4. From an undated entry, estimated c. 1711, in Susanna Wesley's devotional journal. Susanna Wesley, *The Complete Writings*, ed. Charles Wallace Jr. (New York: Oxford University Press, 1997), 225.

5. Barbara R. Duguid, *Extravagant Grace: God's Glory Displayed in Our Weakness* (Phillipsburg, NJ: P&R Publishing, 2013), 30–31.

CHAPTER 6

1. Thank you to my cousin Erin Cooper for pointing out how much shame we experience from the way other women speak about their families.

2. David Powlison, *How Does Sanctification Work?* (Wheaton, IL: Crossway, 2017), 63.

3. "Fueling up with Ethanol," edmunds.com, April 29, 2009, https://www.edmunds.com/fuel-economy/fueling-up-with-ethanol.html.

4. Hannah Anderson, *All That's Good: Recovering the Lost Art of Discernment* (Chicago: Moody, 2018), 53.

5. Elyse Fitzpatrick, *Found in Him: The Joy of the Incarnation and Our Union with Christ* (Wheaton, IL: Crossway, 2013), 152.

CHAPTER 7

1. Jennifer Senior, *All Joy and No Fun: The Paradox of Modern Parenthood* (New York: Harper Collins, 2015), 18.

2. See chapter 1 in my first book, *Unsupermommy,* for more. Maggie Combs, *Unsupermommy: Release Expectations, Embrace Imperfection, and Connect to God's Superpower* (Racine, WI: Broadstreet Publishing Group, 2017).

CHAPTER 8

1. Elisabeth Elliot, *Keep a Quiet Heart* (Grand Rapids, MI: Revell, 1995), 51.

2. John Piper, *God Is the Gospel: Meditations on God's Love as the Gift of Himself* (Wheaton, IL: Crossway Books, 2011), 47.

CHAPTER 9

1. Jim Dwyer, "Confronting a Stranger, for Art," *New York Times*, April 2, 2010, https://www.nytimes.com/2010/04/04/nyregion/04about.html.

2. J. I. Packer, *Keep in Step with the Spirit: Finding Fullness in Our Walk with God* (Grand Rapids, MI: Baker, 2005), 42.

3. Ibid., 43.

4. David Powlison, *How Does Sanctification Work?*, 14.

5. Robert Robinson, "Come, Thou Fount of Every Blessing," 1758, alt. Martin Madan (1760), https://hymnary.org/text/come_thou_fount_of_every_blessing.

6. John MacArthur, *Romans 1–8*, MacArthur New Testament Commentary (Chicago: Moody, 1991), 425–26.

7. Maggie Combs, "5 Bible Study Techniques for Busy Moms," Revive Our Hearts, January 14, 2020, https://www.reviveourhearts.com/true-woman/blog/5-bible-study-techniques-busy-moms/.

CHAPTER 11

1. Elyse Fitzpatrick and Eric Schumacher, *Worthy: Celebrating the Value of Women* (Bloomington, MN: Bethany House, 2020), 32.

2. This concept was one of my biggest takeaways from the Bible study *God of Creation* by Jen Wilkin. Jen Wilkin, "Week Four: Created in the Image of God," in *God of Creation: A Study of Genesis 1–11* (Nashville: Life-Way, 2018), video.

3. Elyse Fitzpatrick, *Found in Him: The Joy of the Incarnation and Our Union with Christ* (Wheaton, IL: Crossway, 2013), 21–22.

4. Elyse Fitzpatrick and Eric Schumacher, *Worthy: Celebrating the Value of Women*, 34.

5. Edward T. Welch, *When People Are Big and God Is Small: Overcoming Peer Pressure, Codependency, and the Fear of Man* (Phillipsburg, NJ: P&R Publishing, 1997), 94.

6. *The 5 Love Languages* by Gary Chapman may be a helpful tool in discerning how God has uniquely created your spouse to give and receive affection.

CHAPTER 12

1. Edward T. Welch, *When People Are Big and God Is Small: Overcoming Peer Pressure, Codependency, and the Fear of Man* (Phillipsburg, NJ: P&R Publishing, 1997), 14.

2. Ibid., 30.

3. Kathryn Jezer-Morton, "Did Moms Exist Before Social Media?," *New York Times*, December 5, 2019, https://www.nytimes.com/2020/04/16/parenting/mommy-influencers.html.

4. Jessica Grose, "The Decade Parents Couldn't Win," *New York Times*, December 25, 2019, https://www.nytimes.com/2019/12/25/parenting/the-decade-parents-couldnt-win.html.

5. Paul David Tripp, *Awe: Why It Matters for Everything We Think, Say, and Do* (Wheaton, IL: Crossway, 2015), 21.

6. Jared C. Wilson, *The Imperfect Disciple: Grace for People Who Can't Get Their Act Together* (Grand Rapids, MI: Baker, 2017), 67.

7. Timothy S. Lane and Paul David Tripp, *How People Change* (Greensboro, NC: New Growth Press, 2008), 14.

8. *Merriam-Webster*, s.v. "diligence," https://www.merriam-webster.com/dictionary/diligence.